EDWARD'S MENAGERIE PRESENTS
A PARTRIDGE IN A PEAR TREE

EDWARD'S MENAGERIE PRESENTS

A PARTRIDGE IN A PEAR TREE

Crochet the 12 Birds of Christmas

New York

CONTENTS

INTRODUCTION 06
MY PROJECT BAG 08
MATERIALS 09
HOW TO USE THE PATTERNS 10
CROCHET BASICS 12
TECHNIQUES 13
FINISHING 20

PROJECTS

FELIX THE RED-LEGGED PARTRIDGE 22
BEATRICE THE TURTLE DOVE 28
RUTH THE FRENCH HEN 34
PETER THE BLACKBIRD 40
GILBERT THE PHEASANT 46
LYDIA THE GOOSE 52

MARGOT THE SWAN	58	ACKNOWLEDGMENTS	94
DELILAH THE CATTLE EGRET	64	ABOUT THE AUTHOR	95
LOIS THE GREAT CORMORANT	70		
AGNES THE HERON	76		
NINA THE SPOON-BILLED SANDPIPER	82		
JOHN THE SPOTTED WOODPECKER	88		

INTRODUCTION

"The Twelve Days of Christmas" is a song that many of us will have learned at school, and my children love nothing more than belting out "five gold rings" for the whole of December.

There is much research and discussion over the symbolism and meaning of the song, and I have chosen to interpret the twelve gifts of true love as birds. From the obvious Partridge in a Pear Tree to the drumming of the Woodpecker, you can crochet your own way through the verses and create your own collection of birds. Enjoy making them to give as gifts, for a stunning festive mantel decoration, or even to hang on wreaths, trees, and shelves around your home.

Edward's Menagerie has been a large part of my life for the last eight years, with daily inspiration provided by the stories of people learning to crochet—it feels like my crochet animal patterns are spreading some happiness all over the world. I am as hooked as everyone else on crocheting the next animal pattern in the collection—and Christmas is one of the best times of year to share some joy with what you can make with, and for, others.

The patterns in this book are designed for you and your friends and family to enjoy and are for private use only. I can't wait to see photos once you start making these, so please don't forget to share them and use the #edsanimals hashtag so that I can enjoy seeing them and you can share in everyone else's crochet adventures too.

Wishing you and your families a very Merry Christmas, and may you have lots of fun making and playing with these birds. **Enjoy.**

MY PROJECT BAG

All the birds in this book are made using TOFT pure wool in a double knitting (DK) weight and a C-2 (3 mm) hook. Each bird weighs around 2–2¾ ounces (60–80 g), and the colors are written on the project pages in order of quantity used within that pattern.

To make all of the birds in this book in TOFT double knitting yarn you will need:

Cream, 7 oz (200 g)
Charcoal, 5¼ oz (150 g)
Oatmeal, 4¼ oz (125 g)
Chestnut, 3½ oz (100 g)
Shale, 3½ oz (100 g)
Camel, 3½ oz (100 g)
Stone, 1¾ oz (50 g)
Black, 1¾ oz (50 g)

Ruby, 1¾ oz (50 g)
Orange, 1¾ oz (50 g)
Yellow, 1¾ oz (50 g)
Fudge, ¾ oz (25 g)
Silver, ¾ oz (25 g)
Steel, ¾ oz (25 g)
Green, ¾ oz (25 g)

MATERIALS

YOU WILL NEED

YARN in appropriate colors and quantities (see individual patterns)

CROCHET HOOK in an appropriate size to match the yarn and your gauge

STUFFING material

SEWING needle

EYES use black yarn as shown or safety eyes as an alternative

SCISSORS

TOFT YARNS

I have had the pleasure of selecting, designing, and manufacturing luxury yarns for the past twelve years, and these birds have been crocheted entirely in TOFT yarn. TOFT yarns are luxury, quality, natural fibers manufactured to my distinctive specifications here in the UK. When crocheted in TOFT yarns, the projects are supple and soft but with a closed fabric to hide the stuffing inside.

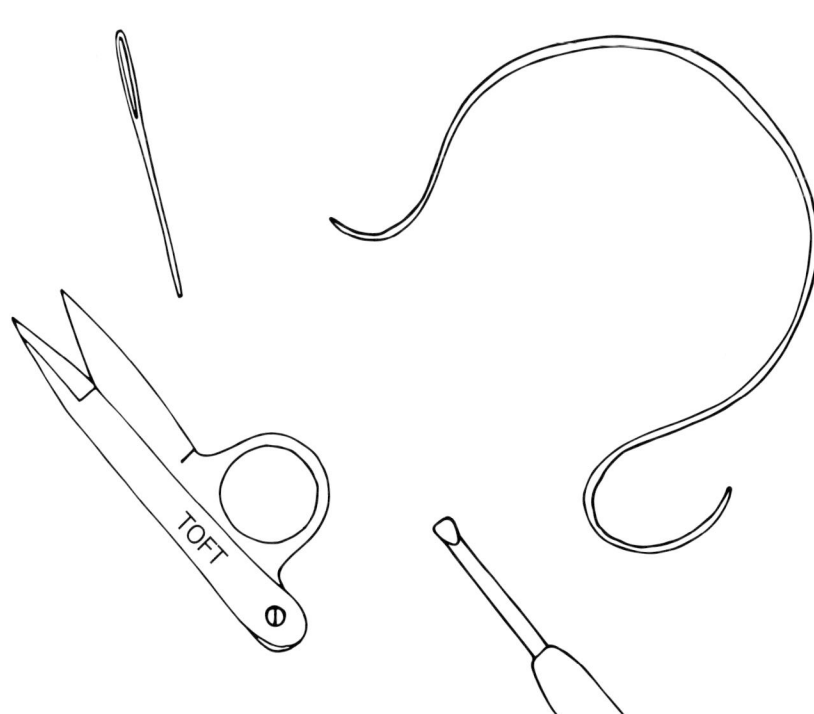

HOW TO USE THE PATTERNS

SKILL LEVELS
The patterns in this book are arranged in order of the song, but each has a SKILL LEVEL to indicate the complexity of the techniques involved.

- **Level one** (beginner) birds are the easiest with the biggest challenge being the splitting technique used for the feet, but everything else should be straightforward once you've learned your single crochet stitch.

- **Level two** (easy) patterns will have more color changing involved in the pattern, but will move cleanly from one yarn to the next at the end of a round.

- **Level three** (intermediate) patterns will require more concentration and include disciplined color changing where you will be moving between two different colored yarns. Mastering the loop stitch will also be required for some of the more advanced projects.

The levels are intended to be encouraging, not off-putting, and serve to ensure that as a newbie to this fun craft, you pick something that will be a bit easier to work as you master counting your stitches, holding your yarn, and remembering to keep track of where you are in the pattern at the same time. I must emphasize that all of the techniques used are easy—the only thing that make some of them very demanding is the discipline involved in accurately counting your way through the pattern. I know when learning to do a new thing, it is nice to be reassured you are not accidentally trying to run before you can walk (but by all means, if you are one of those people who are happy to push themselves, then turn the pages and dive in!).

INTERNATIONAL TERMS
The patterns all use American English crochet terms, primarily the single crochet (UK double crochet) stitch.

SAFETY
Your bird will only be as child-safe as you make it, so don't skimp on the stitches when sewing up. I sew all the way around the edges of any part I am sewing into position. If opting to use safety eyes, buttons, or beads, please be aware that these should not be used on a toy for a child under five years of age. For these young children, you should always embroider the eyes on.

CROCHET BASICS

For more help learning to crochet, see videos at www.toftuk.com.

GAUGE

Edward's Menagerie was inspired by TOFT yarn, and all of the animals in this book have been created in TOFT's pure wool DK yarn and a C-2 (3 mm) hook, but all the patterns will also work with thinner and thicker yarns. The required quantity of yarn needed in the projects is based on using TOFT DK yarns. If using other brands of yarn, the quantities may vary significantly depending on the fiber composition and spinning specifications of the yarn. If you are seeing holes in your fabric when working the patterns, use a hook one size down. Likewise, if your work is too solid and you are finding the stitches hard to work, then use a hook one size up. The standard gauge of TOFT DK yarn on a C-2 (3 mm) hook is 1¼ x 1¼ inches (3 x 3 cm) = 6 sts x 7 rnds.

MARKING

I always view stitch marking as a bit of a lifeline when I crochet. I recommend using a piece of yarn in a contrasting color, approximately 6 inches (15 cm) long, positioned after the end of Round 2; once you have 12 stitches it is easier to see where to place it. As you return back round to your marker, pull it forward or backward through or between your stitches to weave the marker up the fabric. Should you ever complete a round and discover you don't have the correct number of stitches (or even have to abandon what you are making mid-round and forget where you are), you can always return to your last stitch marking.

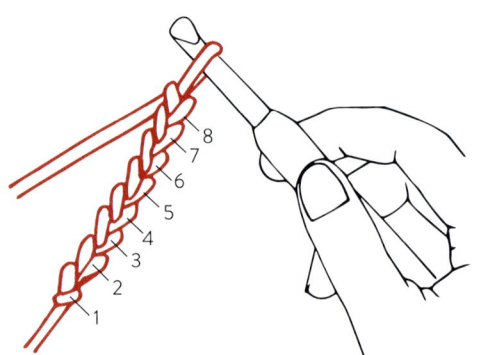

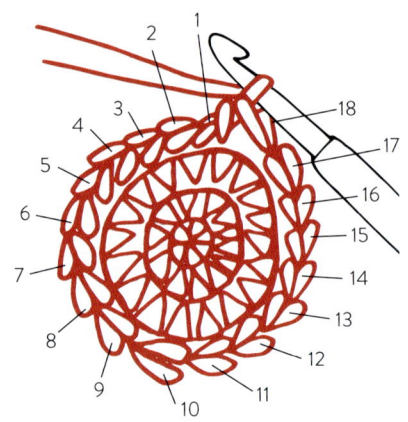

TECHNIQUES

RIGHT-HANDED HOLD

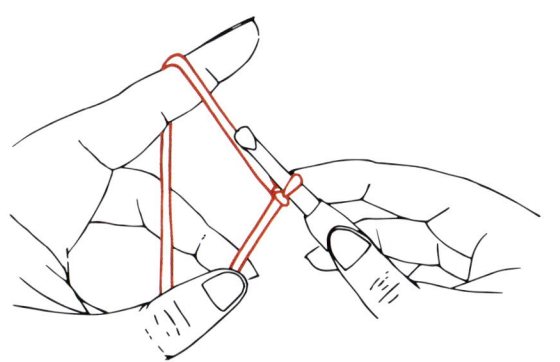

LEFT-HANDED HOLD

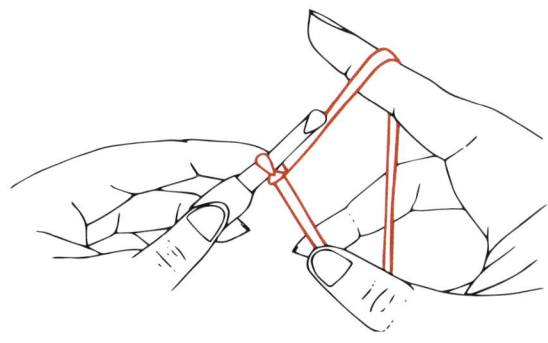

SLIP KNOT

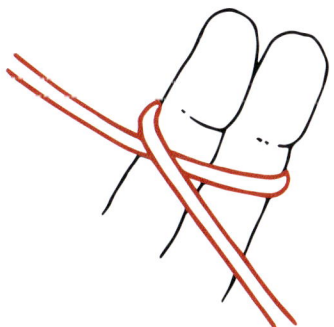

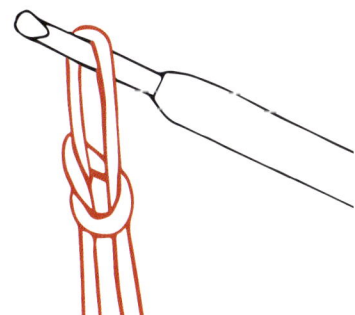

1 Wrap the yarn around your fingers.

2 Pull the tail end of the yarn through the wrapped yarn to make a loop.

3 Place your hook through the loop and tighten, ensuring that it is the tail end of the yarn (not the ball end) that controls the opening and closing of the knot.

CHAIN STITCH (CH)

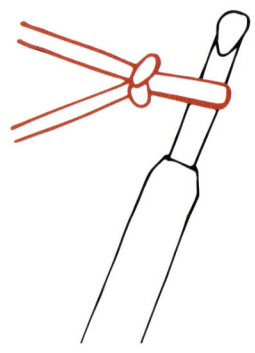
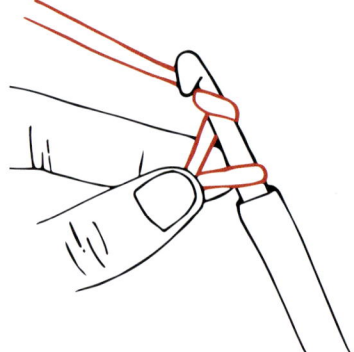
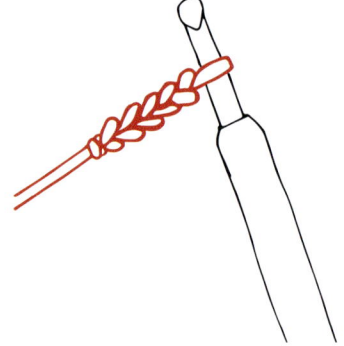

1 Make a slip knot around the hook.

2 Wrap the yarn over the hook (yarn over) and pull it through the loop on the hook.

3 Repeat until you have the desired number of stitches.

SC6 INTO RING (MAGIC CIRCLE)

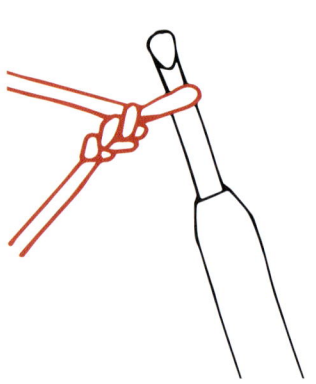
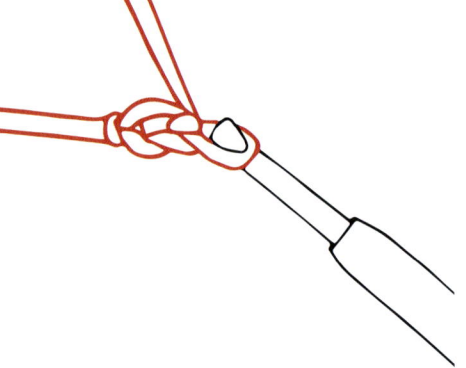
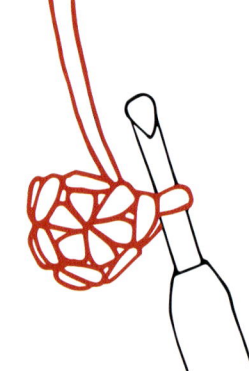

1 Make a slip knot and chain two stitches.

2 Insert the hook into the first chain stitch made and work a single crochet six times into it.

3 Pull tightly on the tail of the yarn to close the center of the ring and form a neat circle.

SINGLE CROCHET STITCH (SC)

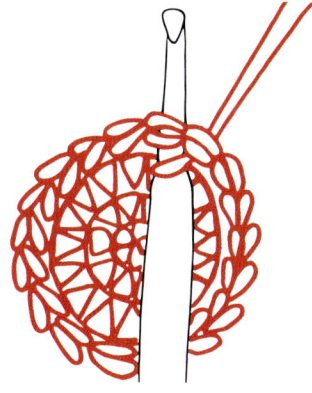 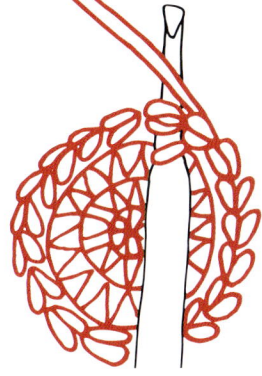 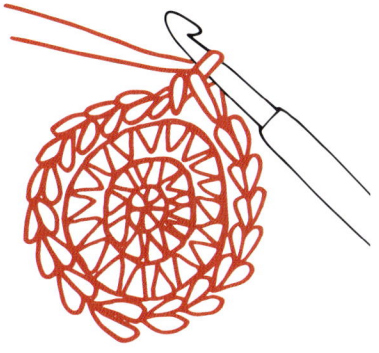

1 Insert the hook through the stitch under both loops of the "V" unless otherwise stated.

2 Yarn over, rotate hook head, and pull through the stitch (two loops on hook).

3 Yarn over again and pull through both loops on the hook to end with one loop on the hook (one single crochet stitch made).

DECREASING (SC2TOG)

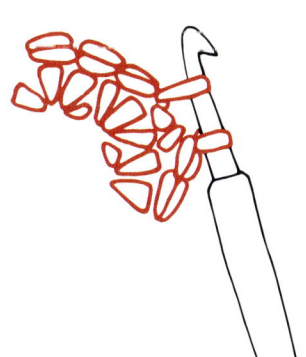 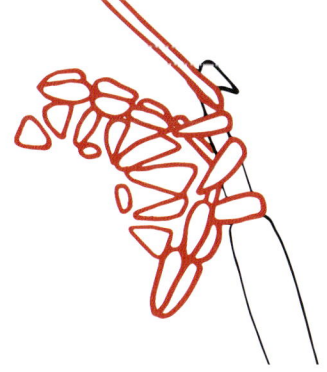 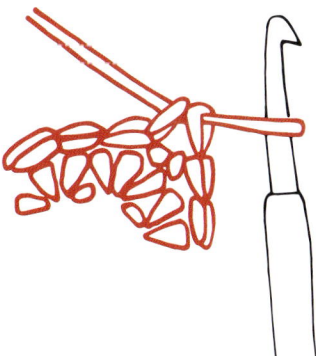

1 Insert the hook under the front loop only of the next stitch (two loops on hook).

2 In the same motion, insert the hook through the front loop only of the following stitch.

3 Yarn over and pull through the first two loops on the hook, then yarn over and pull through both loops.

COLOR CHANGE

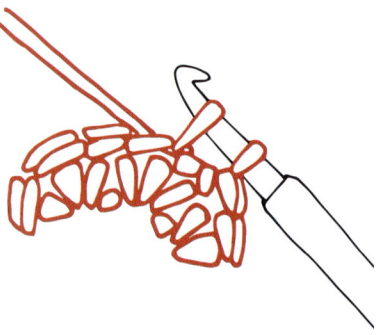 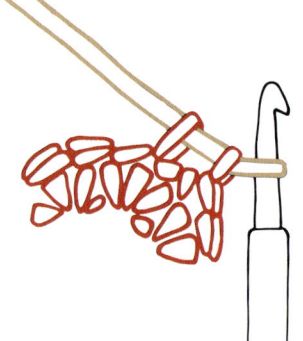 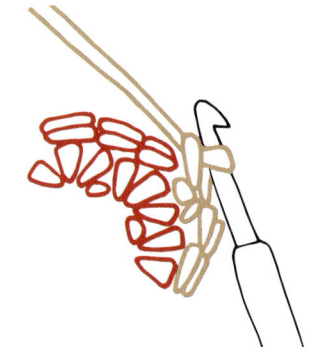

1 Insert the hook through the next stitch, yarn over, and pull through the stitch (two loops on hook).

2 Yarn over with the new color and complete the single crochet stitch with this new yarn.

3 Continue with this new yarn, leaving the original yarn at the back of the work. Cut the original yarn if this is a one-off color change, or run it along the back of the fabric if returning to it later.

SPLITTING THE ROUND

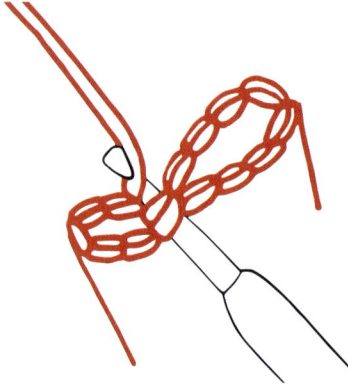 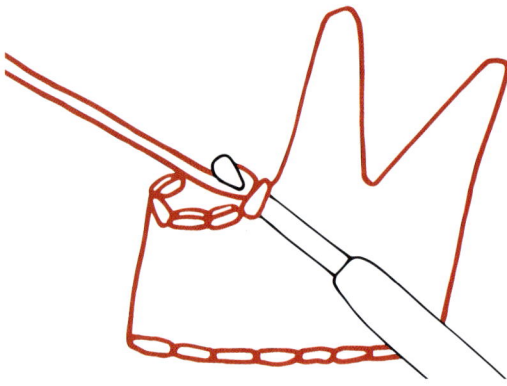

1 Count back the required number of stitches from your hook to split the round as instructed in the pattern. Cross the round and single crochet into this stitch from the right side of the fabric to create two smaller rounds.

2 Work the stitches on the first smaller round as instructed. Once completed, rejoin the yarn and work the other smaller rounds.

CHAIN AND THEN SLIP STITCH TO JOIN INTO CIRCLE

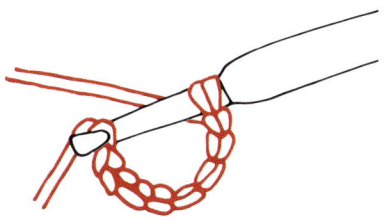 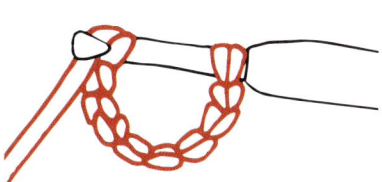 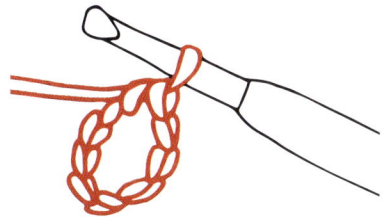

1 Chain the stated number of stitches, then insert the hook into the back of the stitch closest to the slip knot, ensuring not to twist the stitches.

2 Yarn over the hook.

3 Pull the yarn through the stitch and the loop on the hook in one motion.

LOOP STITCH

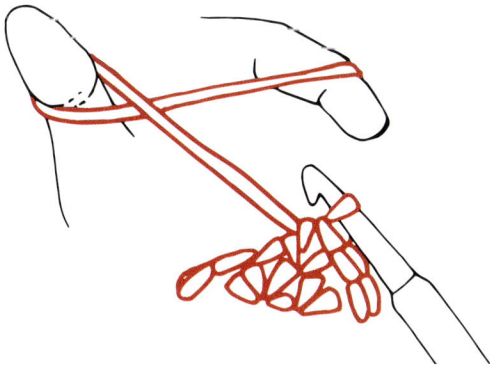 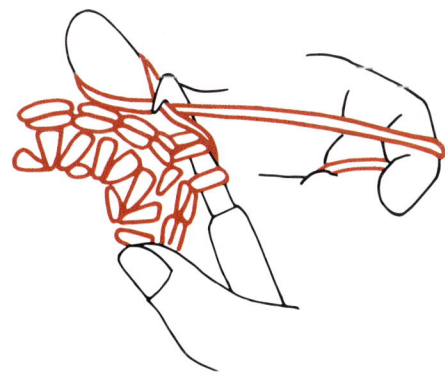

1 Insert the hook through the stitch. Wrap the yarn from front to back over the thumb of your non-hook hand and yarn over with the yarn behind your thumb.

2 Hold the loop on your thumb and complete the single crochet stitch.

SLIP STITCH TRAVERSE

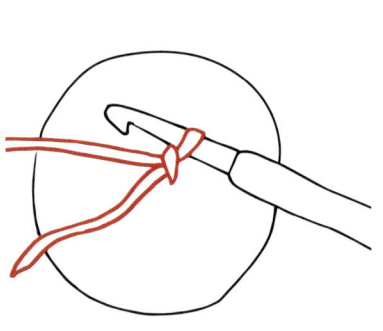 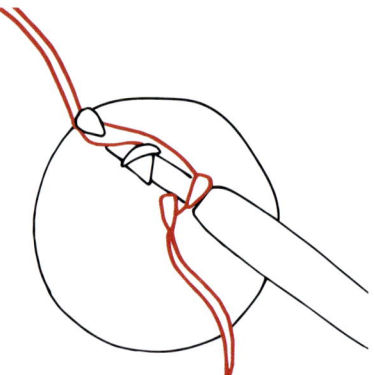 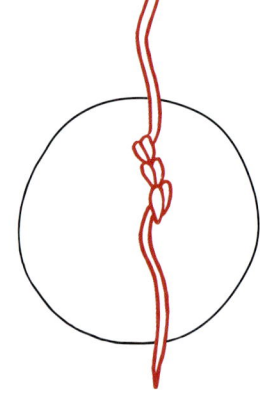

1 Insert the hook into the fabric around a stitch or row.

2 Yarn over and pull through the stitch and all loops on the hook (one slip stitch made).

3 Repeat in desired direction, moving across the surface of the fabric.

CHAIN LOOPS

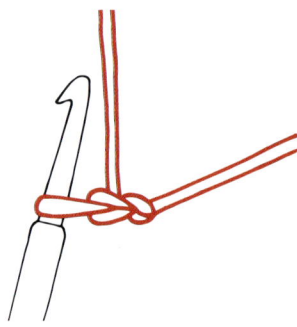 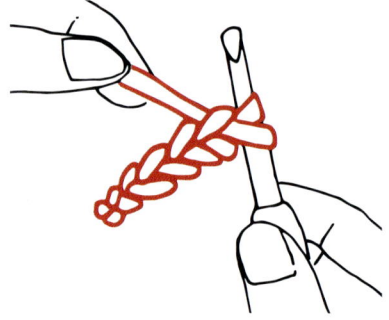 

1 Insert the hook through the fabric at the desired position, yarn over and pull through the fabric.

2 Chain the number of stitches stated in the pattern.

3 Attach the chain to the fabric with a slip stitch approximately two stitches or two rounds away from the start of the chain. Repeat until the required area is covered.

SLIP STITCH CHAINS

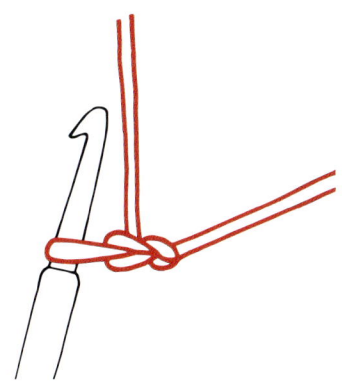 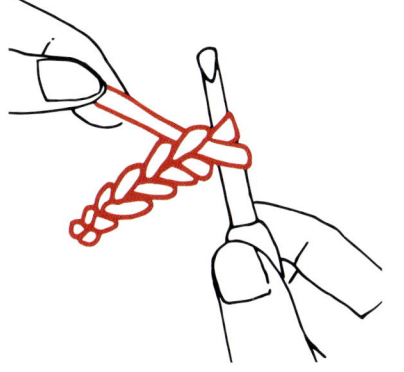 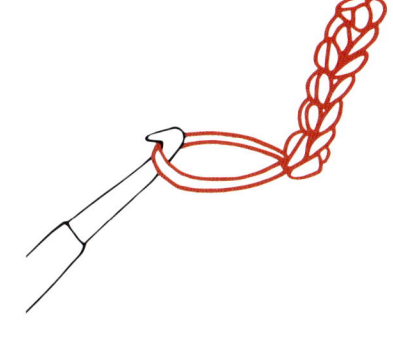

1 Insert the hook through the fabric at the desired position, yarn over and pull through the fabric.

2 Chain the number of stitches stated in the pattern.

3 Working back down the chain, insert the hook into the next stitch.

SLIP STITCH TRAVERSE ROOT

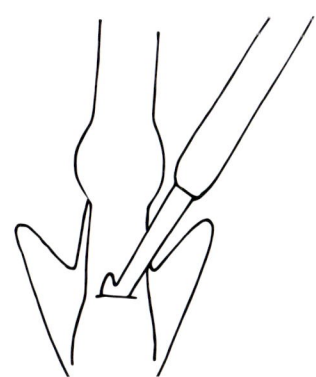 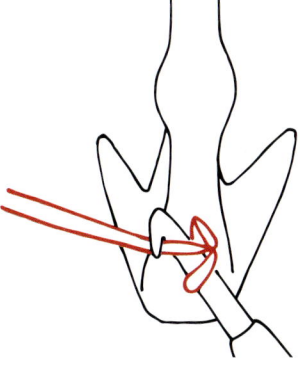 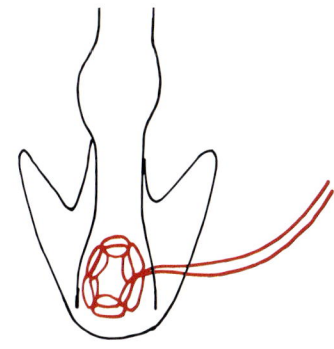

1 Insert hook into the fabric around a st.

2 Yarn over and pull through the loop in one motion (slip stitch).

3 Move across the fabric in a circle making X sts in a round to create a root to then double crochet into.

FINISHING

SEWING UP
To keep each pattern concise, I have omitted all the general stuffing and sewing-up instructions from the pattern if they are common to all. I am not a believer in stuffing the parts as I go along because I find I sometimes then end up working bits of stuffing into my stitches and the added weight of the stuffing impacts my gauge.

When stuffing your birds, less is definitely more. You want to show off the shape of the body and avoid making them firm and stiff, and so proceed with caution and stuff tiny pinches of fluff into the thighs.

STUFFING THE BODIES
All the bodies are stuffed gently to fill out the shape, neck, and chest, but they should retain their supple feel.

STUFFING THE HEADS
All the heads are stuffed at the point at which you decrease to 9 stitches. Any stuffing required in the beaks, crowns, and combs will be detailed in the individual patterns.

STUFFING THE LEGS AND FINISHING THE FEET
While it is not essential to stuff the thighs of any of the birds, on some it will be recommended in the pattern that you do so.

TAILS
Finish the tail by sewing the start of your chain stitch flat and closed and then oversew the tail onto the back horizontally.

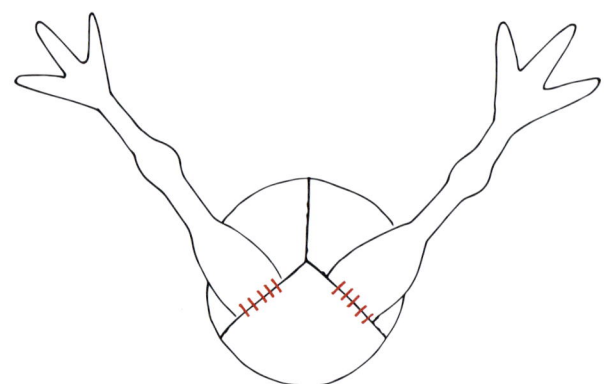

ORDER OF SEWING

Line up the chest shaping and then sew a backstitch to attach the beak to the middle of the face, then follow the steps below:

1. Use backstitches to sew your wings into position in the desired location.
2. Oversew your legs into position (see opposite page).
3. Oversew the flat tail horizontally across back.
4. Add the extras.

1

FELIX
THE RED-LEGGED PARTRIDGE

Having spent twelve months diligently practicing his "ho, ho, ho" every morning in the shower, Felix feels like he has fully rehearsed and ready to become one of Santa's little helpers this year. Although he attempted it, growing a beard beyond a light smattering of stubble proved too much of a challenge, so instead he's heavily invested in a magnificent real yak hair beard, which he's conscientiously oiled to a stunning sheen these last few weeks. Regardless of his suspicions about whether someone may have made it to the Naughty or Nice list, he's got smiles for everyone as he asks all the children what they would like to find under the tree this Christmas.

SKILL LEVEL: INTERMEDIATE **SHALE, CAMEL, RUBY, CREAM, CHARCOAL, CHESTNUT**

BODY/NECK/HEAD
Working in Camel, begin by sc6 into ring.
Rnd 1 (sc2 into next st) 6 times (12 sts)
Rnd 2 (sc1, sc2 into next st) 6 times (18)
Rnd 3 (sc2, sc2 into next st) 6 times (24)
Rnd 4 (sc3, sc2 into next st) 6 times (30)
Rnd 5 (sc4, sc2 into next st) 6 times (36)
Rnd 6 (sc5, sc2 into next st) 6 times (42)
Rnd 7 sc
Change to Shale.
Rnds 8–9 sc (2 rnds)
Rnd 10 (sc5, sc2tog) 6 times (36)
Rnds 11–14 sc (4 rnds)
Rnd 15 (sc4, sc2tog) 6 times (30)
Rnds 16–17 sc (2 rnds)
Change to Cream.
Rnd 18 sc
Rnd 19 (sc4 Cream, sc1 Charcoal) 6 times
Rnd 20 (sc3, sc2tog) 6 times Cream (24)
Rnd 21 sc Cream
Rnd 22 sc3 Cream, sc2tog Charcoal, (sc2tog) 3 times Cream, sc2tog Charcoal, (sc2tog) 3 times Cream, sc2tog Charcoal, sc3 Cream (15)
Rnd 23 (sc2tog) 5 times, sc5 Cream (10)
Change to Charcoal.
Rnd 24 sc
Rnd 25 (sc2 into next st) 10 times (20)
Rnd 26 (sc3, sc2 into next st) 5 times (25)
Rnd 27 (sc4, sc2 into next st) 5 times (30)
Rnd 28 (sc2, sc2 into next st) 10 times (40)
Rnd 29 sc11 Charcoal, sc18 Cream, sc2 Charcoal, sc9 Shale
Rnds 30–32 sc9 Shale, sc2 Charcoal, sc18 Cream, sc2 Charcoal, sc9 Shale (3 rnds)
Rnd 33 sc7, sc2tog Shale, sc2 Charcoal, sc7, sc2tog, sc6, sc2tog Cream, sc2 Charcoal, sc8, sc2tog Shale (36)
Rnd 34 sc4, sc2tog, sc3 Shale, sc2 Charcoal, sc2tog, sc3, sc2tog, sc4, sc2tog, sc2 Cream, sc2 Charcoal, sc2tog, sc4, sc2tog Shale (30)
Rnd 35 sc3, sc2tog, sc3 Shale, sc2 Charcoal, (sc2tog, sc2) 3 times Cream, sc2 Charcoal, sc2tog, sc2, sc2tog Shale (24)
Change to Camel.
Rnd 36 (sc2, sc2tog) 6 times (18)
Rnd 37 sc
Rnd 38 (sc2tog) 9 times (9)
Rnd 39 (sc1, sc2tog) 3 times (6)

LEGS (make two)
Working in Camel, ch12 and sl st to join into a circle.
Rnds 1–3 sc (3 rnds)
Rnd 4 (sc2, sc2tog) 3 times (9)
Rnd 5 (sc1, sc2tog) 3 times (6)
Change to Ruby.
Rnds 6–8 sc (3 rnds)
Rnd 9 (sc2 into next st) 6 times (12)
Rnds 10–11 sc (2 rnds)
Rnd 12 (sc2tog) 6 times (6)
Rnds 13–16 sc (4 rnds)
Rnd 17 (sc2 into next st) 6 times (12)

Rnd 18 (sc1, sc2 into next st) 6 times (18)
Split into three rnds of 6 sts and work each as follows:
Rnds 1–3 sc (3 rnds)
Rnd 4 sc2tog, sc4 (5)
Rnd 5 sc
Rnd 6 sc2tog, sc3 (4)

BACK DIGIT (optional)
SLIP STITCH TRAVERSE (see page 19) a 6-st base on back of foot and work as follows:
Rnd 1 sc
Rnd 2 sc2tog, sc4 (5)
Rnd 3 sc
Rnd 4 sc2tog, sc3 (4)
Lightly stuff thigh and sew flat across top to close.

WINGS (make two)
Working 1 rnd stripes of Cream and Chestnut throughout, begin by sc6 into ring.
Rnd 1 (sc2 into next st) 6 times (12)
Rnd 2 (sc1, sc2 into next st) 6 times (18)
Rnd 3 (sc2, sc2 into next st) 6 times (24)
Rnds 4–5 sc (2 rnds)
Rnd 6 (sc2, sc2tog) 6 times (18)
Rnds 7–8 sc (2 rnds)
Rnd 9 (sc4, sc2tog) 3 times (15)
Rnd 10 sc
Rnd 11 (sc1, sc2tog) 5 times (10)
Rnds 12–13 sc (2 rnds)
Rnd 14 (sc2tog) 5 times (5)
Do not stuff.

BEAK
Working in Ruby, ch12 and sl st to join into a circle.
Rnds 1–2 sc (2 rnds)
Rnd 3 (sc2, sc2tog) 3 times (9)
Rnd 4 (sc1, sc2tog) 3 times (6)
Rnd 5 sc
Rnd 6 (sc2tog) 3 times (3)
Stuff lightly and sew into position.

EYE PATCHES (make two)
Working in Ruby, begin by sc6 into a ring.
Rnd 1 (sc1, sc2 into next st) 3 times (9)
Sew into position.

TAIL
Working in Shale, ch16 and sl st to join into a circle.
Rnd 1 sc
Rnds 2–6 sc (5 rnds)
Split into two rnds of 8 sts and work each as follows:
Rnds 1–4 sc (4 rnds)
Rnd 5 sc7, sc2 into next st (9)
Rnds 6–7 sc (2 rnds)
Rnd 8 (sc2, sc2 into next st) 3 times (12)
Rnds 9–10 sc (2 rnds)
Rnd 11 (sc2, sc2tog) 3 times (9)
Rnd 12 (sc1, sc2tog) 3 times (6)
Do not stuff.

Finish by sewing eyes into place with Black yarn.

2

BEATRICE
THE TURTLE DOVE

Beatrice has twenty-four grandchildren (and that number is not showing any signs of plateauing). Every year since the birth of her first granddaughter she has upheld her own Christmas tradition of knitting each child a new stocking to hang off the mantel. With every new ultrasound scan she's sent to adorn her fridge, her Christmas custom becomes more of a challenge. No longer requiring any kind of pattern, she can turn a heel on anything in a jiffy, mastering cables, Fair Isle, and every other technique she can get her hands on to use for her latest giant sock. If this Christmas brings an announcement of the pitter-patter of tiny feet once again, she might treat herself just to the one week off, before casting on the first one on New Year's Day.

SKILL LEVEL: INTERMEDIATE   **OATMEAL, CAMEL, CHARCOAL, STONE, CREAM**

BODY/NECK/HEAD
Working in Oatmeal, begin by sc6 into ring.
Rnd 1 (sc2 into next st) 6 times (12 sts)
Rnd 2 (sc1, sc2 into next st) 6 times (18)
Rnd 3 (sc2, sc2 into next st) 6 times (24)
Rnd 4 (sc3, sc2 into next st) 6 times (30)
Rnd 5 (sc4, sc2 into next st) 6 times (36)
Rnd 6 (sc5, sc2 into next st) 6 times (42)
Rnds 7–9 sc (3 rnds)
Rnd 10 (sc5, sc2tog) 6 times (36)
Rnds 11–14 sc (4 rnds)
Rnd 15 (sc4, sc2tog) 6 times (30)
Rnds 16–19 sc (4 rnds)
Rnd 20 (sc3, sc2tog) 6 times (24)
Rnd 21 sc
Stuff and continue.
Rnd 22 (sc2tog) 9 times Oatmeal, sc6 Cream (15)
Rnd 23 (sc2tog) 4 times Oatmeal, sc2tog, sc5 Charcoal (10)
Rnd 24 sc1 Charcoal, sc4 Oatmeal, sc5 Cream
Rnd 25 sc1 into next st Cream, sc1 into same st Oatmeal, (sc2 into next st) 4 times Oatmeal, (sc2 into next st) 5 times Charcoal (20)
Rnd 26 sc2 Charcoal, sc1, sc2 into next st, sc3, sc2 into next st, sc2 Oatmeal, sc1, sc2 into next st, (sc3, sc2 into next st) twice Cream (25)
Rnd 27 sc3 Cream, sc1, sc2 into next st, sc4, sc2 into next st, sc2 Oatmeal, sc2, sc2 into next st, (sc4, sc2 into next st) twice Charcoal (30)
Rnd 28 sc2, sc2 into next st Charcoal, (sc2, sc2 into next st) 9 times Oatmeal (40)
Continue in Oatmeal.

Rnds 29–31 sc (3 rnds)
Rnd 32 (sc8, sc2tog) 4 times (36)
Rnd 33 sc
Rnd 34 (sc4, sc2tog) 6 times (30)
Rnd 35 (sc3, sc2tog) 6 times (24)
Rnd 36 (sc2, sc2tog) 6 times (18)
Rnd 37 sc
Rnd 38 (sc2tog) 9 times (9)
Rnd 39 (sc1, sc2tog) 3 times (6)

LEGS (make two)
Working in Oatmeal, ch12 and sl st to join into a circle.
Rnds 1–3 sc (3 rnds)
Rnd 4 (sc2, sc2tog) 3 times (9)
Rnd 5 (sc1, sc2tog) 3 times (6)
Change to Stone.
Rnds 6–11 sc (6 rnds)
Rnd 12 (sc2 into next st) 6 times (12)
Rnds 13–14 sc (2 rnds)
Rnd 15 (sc2tog) 6 times (6)
Rnds 16–22 sc (7 rnds)
Rnd 23 (sc2 into next st) 6 times (12)
Rnd 24 (sc1, sc2 into next st) 6 times (18)
Split into three rnds of 6 sts and work each as follows:
Rnds 1–3 sc (3 rnds)
Rnd 4 sc2tog, sc4 (5)
Rnds 5–6 sc (2 rnds)
Rnd 7 sc2tog, sc3 (4)

BACK DIGIT (optional)
SLIP STITCH TRAVERSE (see page 19) a 6-st root on back of foot and work as follows:
Rnd 1 sc
Rnd 2 sc2tog, sc4 (5)
Rnds 3–4 sc (2 rnds)
Rnd 5 sc2tog, sc3 (4)
Lightly stuff thigh and sew flat across top to close.

WINGS (make two)
Working in Charcoal, begin by sc6 into ring.
Rnd 1 (sc1, sc2 into next st) 3 times (9)
Rnd 2 sc8, sc2 into next st (10)
Rnd 3 sc
Rnd 4 sc9, sc2 into next st (11)
Rnd 5 sc
Rnd 6 sc10, sc2 into next st (12)
Change to working odd rnds in Camel and even rnds as 2 sts Camel, 2 sts Charcoal.
Rnd 7 sc
Rnd 8 sc11, sc2 into next st (13)
Rnd 9 sc
Rnd 10 sc12, sc2 into next st (14)
Rnd 11 sc
Rnd 12 (sc6, sc2 into next st) twice (16)
Rnd 13 sc2 into next st, sc14, sc2 into next st (18)
Rnd 14 sc2 into next st, sc16, sc2 into next st (20)
Rnd 15 sc2 into next st, sc18, sc2 into next st (22)
Rnd 16 sc2 into next st, sc20, sc2 into next st (24)
Rnd 17 sc2 into next st, sc22, sc2 into next st (26)
Rnds 18–21 sc (4 rnds)
Rnd 22 (sc11, sc2tog) twice (24)
Rnd 23 (sc2, sc2tog) 6 times (18)
Rnd 24 sc
Rnd 25 (sc1, sc2tog) 6 times (12)
Rnd 26 (sc2tog) 6 times (6)
Do not stuff.

BEAK
Working in Stone, ch8 and sl st to join into a circle.
Rnds 1–2 sc (2 rnds)
Rnd 3 (sc2, sc2tog) twice (6)
Rnds 4–5 sc (2 rnds)
Rnd 6 (sc2tog) 3 times (3)
Stuff lightly and sew into position.

TAIL
Working in Oatmeal, ch16 and sl st to join into a circle.
Rnds 1–5 sc (5 rnds)
Change to Charcoal.
Rnd 6 sc
Change to Camel.
Split into two rnds of 8 sts and work each as follows:
Rnds 1–3 sc (3 rnds)
Change to Charcoal.
Rnd 4 sc
Change to Camel.
Rnd 5 sc7, sc2 into next st (9)
Rnds 6–7 sc (2 rnds)
Continue in Charcoal.
Rnd 8 sc8, sc2 into next st (10)
Rnds 9–10 sc (2 rnds)
Rnd 11 (sc4, sc2 into next st) twice (12)
Rnds 12–13 sc (2 rnds)
Rnd 14 (sc2tog) 6 times (6)
Do not stuff.

Finish by sewing eyes into place with Black yarn.

3

RUTH
THE FRENCH HEN

Ruth is adamant that this is the year she will finally perfect her eggnog technique and blow her neighbors away with the ultimate festive party drink. She's whisking and folding her way to success, while filling her house with all her favorite smells of cloves, nutmeg, cinnamon, and vanilla. Ruth likes her eggnog to embody the warmth of a family Christmas around an open fire, so she likes hers with bourbon. But to please everyone, she has combined her frothy Christmas cloud with three different spirits. With that all sorted, there's just enough time for her pick out her most glitzy outfit, pour the snacks into bowls, and get ready to wish everyone a very Merry Christmas.

SKILL LEVEL: BEGINNER **OATMEAL, CAMEL**

BODY/NECK/HEAD
Working in Oatmeal, begin by sc6 into ring.
Rnd 1 (sc2 into next st) 6 times (12 sts)
Rnd 2 (sc1, sc2 into next st) 6 times (18)
Rnd 3 (sc2, sc2 into next st) 6 times (24)
Rnd 4 (sc3, sc2 into next st) 6 times (30)
Rnd 5 (sc4, sc2 into next st) 6 times (36)
Rnd 6 (sc5, sc2 into next st) 6 times (42)
Rnds 7–9 sc (3 rnds)
Rnd 10 (sc5, sc2tog) 6 times (36)
Rnds 11–14 sc (4 rnds)
Rnd 15 (sc4, sc2tog) 6 times (30)
Rnds 16–19 sc (4 rnds)
Rnd 20 (sc3, sc2tog) 6 times (24)
Rnd 21 sc
Rnd 22 (sc2tog) 9 times, sc6 (15)
Rnd 23 (sc2tog) 5 times, sc5 (10)
Rnd 24 sc
Rnd 25 (sc2 into next st) 10 times (20)
Rnd 26 (sc3, sc2 into next st) 5 times (25)
Rnd 27 (sc4, sc2 into next st) 5 times (30)
Rnd 28 (sc2, sc2 into next st) 10 times (40)
Rnds 29–31 sc (3 rnds)
Rnd 32 (sc8, sc2tog) 4 times (36)
Rnd 33 sc
Rnd 34 (sc4, sc2tog) 6 times (30)
Rnd 35 (sc3, sc2tog) 6 times (24)
Rnd 36 (sc2, sc2tog) 6 times (18)
Rnd 37 sc
Rnd 38 (sc2tog) 9 times (9)
Rnd 39 (sc1, sc2tog) 3 times (6)

LEGS (make two)
Working in Oatmeal, ch12 and sl st to join into a circle.
Rnds 1–3 sc (3 rnds)
Rnd 4 (sc2, sc2tog) 3 times (9)
Rnd 5 (sc1, sc2tog) 3 times (6)
Change to Camel.
Rnds 6–12 sc (7 rnds)
Rnd 13 (sc2 into next st) 6 times (12)
Rnds 14–15 sc (2 rnds)
Rnd 16 (sc2tog) 6 times (6)
Rnds 17–24 sc (8 rnds)
Rnd 25 (sc2 into next st) 6 times (12)
Rnd 26 (sc1, sc2 into next st) 6 times (18)
Split into three rnds of 6 sts and work each as follows:
Rnds 1–3 sc (3 rnds)
Rnd 4 sc2tog, sc4 (5)
Rnds 5–6 sc (2 rnds)
Rnd 7 sc2tog, sc3 (4)

BACK DIGIT (optional)
SLIP STITCH TRAVERSE (see page 19) a 6-st root on back of foot and work as follows:
Rnd 1 sc
Rnd 2 sc2tog, sc4 (5)
Rnds 3–4 sc (2 rnds)
Rnd 5 sc2tog, sc3 (4)
Lightly stuff thigh and sew flat across top to close.

WINGS (make two)
Working in Oatmeal, begin by sc6 into ring.
Rnd 1 (sc1, sc2 into next st) 3 times (9)
Rnd 2 sc8, sc2 into next st (10)
Rnd 3 sc
Rnd 4 sc9, sc2 into next st (11)
Rnd 5 sc
Rnd 6 sc10, sc2 into next st (12)
Rnd 7 sc
Rnd 8 sc11, sc2 into next st (13)
Rnd 9 sc
Rnd 10 sc12, sc2 into next st (14)
Rnd 11 sc
Rnd 12 (sc6, sc2 into next st) twice (16)
Rnd 13 sc2 into next st, sc14, sc2 into next st (18)
Rnd 14 sc2 into next st, sc16, sc2 into next st (20)
Rnd 15 sc2 into next st, sc18, sc2 into next st (22)
Rnd 16 sc2 into next st, sc20, sc2 into next st (24)
Rnd 17 sc2 into next st, sc22, sc2 into next st (26)
Rnds 18–21 sc (4 rnds)
Rnd 22 (sc11, sc2tog) twice (24)
Rnd 23 (sc2, sc2tog) 6 times (18)
Rnd 24 sc
Rnd 25 (sc1, sc2tog) 6 times (12)
Rnd 26 (sc2tog) 6 times (6)
Do not stuff.

BEAK
Working in Camel, ch8 and sl st to join into circle.
Rnds 1–2 sc (2 rnds)
Rnd 3 (sc2, sc2tog) twice (6)
Rnds 4–5 sc (2 rnds)
Rnd 6 (sc1, sc2tog) twice (4)
Stuff lightly and sew into position.

CREST
Working in Oatmeal, work ch15 CHAIN LOOPS (see page 18) over top of the head.

TAIL
Working in Oatmeal, work two rows of four ch24 CHAIN LOOPS in tail position.

Finish by sewing eyes into place with Black yarn.

4

PETER
THE BLACKBIRD

You know that guy who always jokes about starting his shopping at lunchtime on Christmas Eve? Peter is that guy. It potentially goes some way toward explaining why he's yet to find a long-term mate. He's been looking for a while for someone who will laugh with him at his haphazard gifting, which probably has a 50/50 rate of blinding success or crushing failure. He'd be happy to find someone who tolerates the task of earmarking their own gift in early November (and accepting that if they don't select that gift wrapping option, they'll have to make a choice between doing it themselves or finding a box decorated with warehouse barcodes instead of ribbons under the tree!).

SKILL LEVEL: BEGINNER **CHARCOAL, YELLOW**

BODY/NECK/HEAD
Working in Charcoal, begin by sc6 into ring.
Rnd 1 (sc2 into next st) 6 times (12 sts)
Rnd 2 (sc1, sc2 into next st) 6 times (18)
Rnd 3 (sc2, sc2 into next st) 6 times (24)
Rnd 4 (sc3, sc2 into next st) 6 times (30)
Rnd 5 (sc4, sc2 into next st) 6 times (36)
Rnd 6 (sc5, sc2 into next st) 6 times (42)
Rnds 7–9 sc (3 rnds)
Rnd 10 (sc5, sc2tog) 6 times (36)
Rnds 11–14 sc (4 rnds)
Rnd 15 (sc4, sc2tog) 6 times (30)
Rnds 16–19 sc (4 rnds)
Rnd 20 (sc3, sc2tog) 6 times (24)
Rnd 21 sc
Rnd 22 (sc2tog) 9 times, sc6 (15)
Rnd 23 (sc2tog) 5 times, sc5 (10)
Stuff and continue.
Rnd 24 sc
Rnd 25 (sc2 into next st) 10 times (20)
Rnd 26 (sc3, sc2 into next st) 5 times (25)
Rnd 27 (sc4, sc2 into next st) 5 times (30)
Rnd 28 (sc2, sc2 into next st) 10 times (40)
Rnds 29–31 sc (3 rnds)
Rnd 32 (sc8, sc2tog) 4 times (36)
Rnd 33 sc
Rnd 34 (sc4, sc2tog) 6 times (30)
Rnd 35 (sc3, sc2tog) 6 times (24)
Rnd 36 (sc2, sc2tog) 6 times (18)
Rnd 37 sc
Rnd 38 (sc2tog) 9 times (9)
Rnd 39 (sc1, sc2tog) 3 times (6)

LEGS (make two)
Working in Charcoal, ch12 and sl st to join into a circle.
Rnds 1–3 sc (3 rnds)
Rnd 4 (sc2, sc2tog) 3 times (9)
Rnd 5 (sc1, sc2tog) 3 times (6)
Change to Yellow.
Rnds 6–12 sc (7 rnds)
Rnd 13 (sc2 into next st) 6 times (12)
Rnds 14–15 sc (2 rnds)
Rnd 16 (sc2tog) 6 times (6)
Rnds 17–24 sc (8 rnds)
Rnd 25 (sc2 into next st) 6 times (12)
Rnd 26 (sc1, sc2 into next st) 6 times (18)
Split into three rnds of 6 sts and work each as follows:
Rnds 1–3 sc (3 rnds)
Rnd 4 sc2tog, sc4 (5)
Rnds 5–6 sc (2 rnds)
Rnd 7 sc2tog, sc3 (4)

BACK DIGIT (optional)
SLIP STITCH TRAVERSE (see page 19) a 6-st root on back of foot and work as follows:
Rnd 1 sc
Rnd 2 sc2tog, sc4 (5)
Rnds 3–4 sc (2 rnds)
Rnd 5 sc2tog, sc3 (4)
Lightly stuff thigh and sew flat across top to close.

WINGS (make two)
Working in Charcoal, begin by sc6 into ring.
Rnd 1 (sc1, sc2 into next st) 3 times (9)
Rnd 2 sc8, sc2 into next st (10)
Rnd 3 sc
Rnd 4 sc9, sc2 into next st (11)
Rnd 5 sc
Rnd 6 sc10, sc2 into next st (12)
Rnd 7 sc
Rnd 8 sc11, sc2 into next st (13)
Rnd 9 sc
Rnd 10 sc12, sc2 into next st (14)
Rnd 11 sc
Rnd 12 (sc6, sc2 into next st) twice (16)
Rnd 13 sc2 into next st, sc14, sc2 into next st (18)
Rnd 14 sc2 into next st, sc16, sc2 into next st (20)
Rnd 15 sc2 into next st, sc18, sc2 into next st (22)
Rnd 16 sc2 into next st, sc20, sc2 into next st (24)
Rnd 17 sc2 into next st, sc22, sc2 into next st (26)
Rnds 18–21 sc (4 rnds)
Rnd 22 (sc11, sc2tog) twice (24)
Rnd 23 (sc2, sc2tog) 6 times (18)
Rnd 24 sc
Rnd 25 (sc1, sc2tog) 6 times (12)
Rnd 26 (sc2tog) 6 times (6)
Do not stuff.

BEAK
Working in Yellow, ch8 and sl st to join into a circle.
Rnd 1 sc
Rnd 2 (sc2, sc2tog) twice (6)
Rnds 3–4 sc (2 rnds)
Rnd 5 (sc1, sc2tog) twice (4)
Rnd 6 (sc2tog) twice (2)
Stuff lightly and sew into position.

TAIL
Working in Charcoal, ch16 and sl st to join into a circle.
Rnds 1–6 sc (6 rnds)
Split into two rnds of 8 sts and work each as follows:
Rnds 1–4 sc (4 rnds)
Rnd 5 sc7, sc2 into next st (9)
Rnds 6–8 sc (3 rnds)
Rnd 9 sc8, sc2 into next st (10)
Rnds 10–12 sc (3 rnds)
Rnd 13 (sc3, sc2tog) twice (8)
Rnd 14 (sc2, sc2tog) twice (6)
Rnd 15 (sc2tog) 3 times (3)

Finish by sewing eyes into place with Black yarn.

15

GILBERT
THE PHEASANT

There's no better time of year to be in a church choir than when you get to swap the hymns for carols, put your Christmas sweater on, and get ready to be jolly. Gilbert's never happier than when he's simultaneously eating cake and belting out his "fa-la-la-la-laaas" as loud as his lungs will allow (and that tends to be for most of the festive period). He spends Christmas fueled by mince pies, panettone, and Yule logs, moving energetically from one sugar high to the next. Knowing of his fondness for festive puddings, his late great-aunt passed down her handwritten recipe book. For many years now, he has spent a whole Sunday humming all his favorite "pa-rup-a-pum-pums" as he bakes until he drops.

SKILL LEVEL: INTERMEDIATE

CHESTNUT, CAMEL, OATMEAL, ORANGE, GREEN, FUDGE

SPOT PATTERN
Work 3 sts Camel, 2 sts Chestnut.

BODY/NECK/HEAD
Working in SPOT PATTERN, begin by sc6 into ring.
Rnd 1 (sc2 into next st) 6 times (12 sts)
Rnd 2 (sc1, sc2 into next st) 6 times (18)
Rnd 3 (sc2, sc2 into next st) 6 times (24)
Rnd 4 (sc3, sc2 into next st) 6 times (30)
Rnd 5 (sc4, sc2 into next st) 6 times (36)
Rnd 6 (sc5, sc2 into next st) 6 times (42)
Rnds 7–9 sc (3 rnds)
Rnd 10 (sc5, sc2tog) 6 times (36)
Rnds 11–14 sc (4 rnds)
Rnd 15 (sc4, sc2tog) 6 times (30)
Change to working odd rnds in SPOT PATTERN and even rnds as 2 sts Camel, 2 sts Chestnut.
Rnds 16–19 sc (4 rnds)
Rnd 20 (sc3, sc2tog) 6 times (24)
Rnd 21 sc
Change to Oatmeal.
Rnd 22 (sc2tog) 9 times, sc6 (15)
Rnd 23 (sc2tog) 5 times, sc5 (10)
Change to Green.
Rnd 24 sc
Rnd 25 (sc2 into next st) 5 times Orange, (sc2 into next st) 5 times Green (20)
Rnd 26 (sc3, sc2 into next st) twice, sc2 Orange, sc1, sc2 into next st, (sc3, sc2 into next st) twice Green (25)
Rnd 27 (sc4, sc2 into next st) twice, sc2 Orange, sc2, sc2 into next st, (sc4, sc2 into next st) twice Green (30)
Rnd 28 (sc2, sc2 into next st) 4 times, sc2 Orange, sc2 into next st, (sc2, sc2 into next st) 5 times Green (40)
Rnds 29–31 sc18 Orange, sc22 Green (3 rnds)
Rnd 32 sc8, sc2tog, sc8 Orange, sc2tog, (sc8, sc2tog) twice Green (36)
Rnd 33 sc17 Orange, sc19 Green
Rnd 34 (sc4, sc2tog) 3 times Orange, (sc4, sc2tog) 3 times Green (30)
Continue in Green.
Rnd 35 (sc3, sc2tog) 6 times (24)
Rnd 36 (sc2, sc2tog) 6 times (18)
Rnd 37 sc
Rnd 38 (sc2tog) 9 times (9)
Rnd 39 (sc1, sc2tog) 3 times (6)

LEGS (make two)
Working in Chestnut, ch12 and sl st to join into a circle.
Rnds 1–3 sc (3 rnds)
Rnd 4 (sc2, sc2tog) 3 times (9)
Rnd 5 (sc1, sc2tog) 3 times (6)
Change to Oatmeal.
Rnds 6–11 sc (6 rnds)
Rnd 12 (sc2 into next st) 6 times (12)
Rnds 13–14 sc (2 rnds)
Rnd 15 (sc2tog) 6 times (6)
Rnds 16–22 sc (7 rnds)
Rnd 23 (sc2 into next st) 6 times (12)
Rnd 24 (sc1, sc2 into next st) 6 times (18)
Split into three rnds of 6 sts and work each as follows:
Rnds 1–3 sc (3 rnds)
Rnd 4 sc2tog, sc4 (5)

Rnds 5–6 sc (2 rnds)
Rnd 7 sc2tog, sc3 (4)

BACK DIGIT (optional)
SLIP STITCH TRAVERSE (see page 19) a 6-st root on back of foot and work as follows:
Rnd 1 sc
Rnd 2 sc2tog, sc4 (5)
Rnds 3–4 sc (2 rnds)
Rnd 5 sc2tog, sc3 (4)
Lightly stuff thigh and sew flat across top to close.

WINGS (make two)
Working in Chestnut, begin by sc6 into ring.
Rnd 1 (sc2 into next st) 6 times (12)
Rnd 2 (sc1, sc2 into next st) 6 times (18)
Rnd 3 (sc2, sc2 into next st) 6 times (24)
Rnds 4–5 sc (2 rnds)
Rnd 6 (sc2, sc2tog) 6 times (18)
Rnds 7–8 sc (2 rnds)
Rnd 9 (sc4, sc2tog) 3 times (15)
Rnd 10 sc
Rnd 11 (sc1, sc2tog) 5 times (10)
Rnds 12–13 sc (2 rnds)
Rnd 14 (sc2tog) 5 times (5)
Do not stuff.

BEAK
Working in Oatmeal, ch8 and sl st to join into a circle.
Rnds 1–2 sc (2 rnds)
Rnd 3 sc6, sc2tog (7)
Rnd 4 sc5, sc2tog (6)
Rnd 5 sc4, sc2tog (5)
Rnd 6 sc
Rnd 7 sc3, sc2tog (4)
Rnd 8 sc2, sc2tog (3)
Stuff lightly and sew into position.

TAIL
Working in Oatmeal with 1 rnd Fudge stripe every 4th rnd throughout, ch16 and sl st to join into a circle.
Rnds 1–6 sc (6 rnds)
Split into two rnds of 8 sts and work each as follows:
Rnds 1–7 sc (7 rnds)
Rnd 8 sc7, sc2 into next st (9)
Rnds 9–14 sc (6 rnds)
Rnd 15 sc8, sc2 into next st (10)
Rnds 16–18 sc (3 rnds)
Rnd 19 (sc3, sc2tog) twice (8)
Rnd 20 (sc2, sc2tog) twice (6)
Rnd 21 (sc2tog) 3 times (3)
Rnd 22 sc2tog, sc1 (2)
Do not stuff.
Sew into alert position by sewing base of tail flat against back of body.

Finish by sewing eyes into place with Black yarn.

6

LYDIA
THE GOOSE

Lydia's feeling anxious this Christmas, but thankfully she has very little left to do to feather the nest while she counts down to her due date. Although at first she was shocked to hear she was expecting her baby on the 25th of December, she's since grown very fond of the idea of a very special present arriving that day. Her mind is filling the hours, rattling through long lists of festive names that might be perfect once she first takes her baby under her wing. With just days to go, this very organized goose already cooked the ham and all the trimmings last week, and has it all safely in her freezer to ensure that whatever happens she won't miss her Christmas dinner!

SKILL LEVEL: EASY   **SHALE, ORANGE, CHARCOAL**

BODY/NECK/HEAD
Working in Shale, begin by sc6 into ring.
Rnd 1 (sc2 into next st) 6 times (12 sts)
Rnd 2 (sc1, sc2 into next st) 6 times (18)
Rnd 3 (sc2, sc2 into next st) 6 times (24)
Rnd 4 (sc3, sc2 into next st) 6 times (30)
Rnd 5 (sc4, sc2 into next st) 6 times (36)
Rnd 6 (sc5, sc2 into next st) 6 times (42)
Rnds 7–9 sc (3 rnds)
Rnd 10 (sc5, sc2tog) 6 times (36)
Rnds 11–14 sc (4 rnds)
Rnd 15 (sc4, sc2tog) 6 times (30)
Rnds 16–19 sc (4 rnds)
Rnd 20 (sc3, sc2tog) 6 times (24)
Rnd 21 sc
Rnd 22 (sc2tog) 9 times, sc6 (15)
Rnd 23 (sc2tog) 5 times, sc5 (10)
Stuff and continue.
Rnds 24–29 sc (6 rnds)
Rnd 30 (sc2 into next st) 10 times (20)
Rnd 31 (sc3, sc2 into next st) 5 times (25)
Rnd 32 (sc4, sc2 into next st) 5 times (30)
Rnd 33 (sc2, sc2 into next st) 10 times (40)
Rnds 34–36 sc (3 rnds)
Rnd 37 (sc8, sc2tog) 4 times (36)
Rnd 38 sc
Rnd 39 (sc4, sc2tog) 6 times (30)
Rnd 40 (sc3, sc2tog) 6 times (24)
Rnd 41 (sc2, sc2tog) 6 times (18)
Rnd 42 sc

Rnd 43 (sc2tog) 9 times (9)
Rnd 44 (sc1, sc2tog) 3 times (6)

LEGS (make two)
Working in Shale, ch16 and sl st to join into a circle.
Rnds 1–5 sc (5 rnds)
Rnd 6 (sc2, sc2tog) 4 times (12)
Rnd 7 (sc1, sc2tog) 4 times (8)
Change to Orange.
Rnds 8–9 sc (2 rnds)
Rnd 10 (sc1, sc2 into next st) 4 times (12)
Rnds 11–12 sc (2 rnds)
Rnd 13 (sc1, sc2tog) 4 times (8)
Rnds 14–20 sc (7 rnds)
Rnd 21 (sc2 into next st) 8 times (16)
Rnd 22 sc
Rnd 23 (sc7, sc2 into next st) twice (18)
Rnd 24 (sc8, sc2 into next st) twice (20)
Rnd 25 sc
Rnd 26 (sc9, sc2 into next st) twice (22)
Rnd 27 sc
Rnd 28 (sc10, sc2 into next st) twice (24)
Rnds 29–31 sc (3 rnds)
Split into three rnds of 8 sts and work each as follows:
Rnd 1 sc
Rnd 2 (sc2tog) 4 times (4)
Rnd 3 (sc2tog) twice (2)
Lightly stuff thigh and sew flat across top to close.

WINGS (make two)
Working in Charcoal, begin by sc6 into ring.
Rnd 1 (sc1, sc2 into next st) 3 times (9)
Rnd 2 sc8, sc2 into next st (10)
Change to Shale.
Rnd 3 sc
Rnd 4 sc9, sc2 into next st (11)
Change to Charcoal.
Rnd 5 sc
Rnd 6 sc10, sc2 into next st (12)
Change to Shale.
Rnd 7 sc
Rnd 8 sc11, sc2 into next st (13)
Change to Charcoal.
Rnd 9 sc
Rnd 10 sc12, sc2 into next st (14)
Change to Shale.
Rnd 11 sc
Rnd 12 (sc6, sc2 into next st) twice (16)
Rnd 13 sc2 into next st, sc14, sc2 into next st (18)
Change to Charcoal.
Rnd 14 sc2 into next st, sc16, sc2 into next st (20)
Change to Shale.
Rnd 15 sc2 into next st, sc18, sc2 into next st (22)
Rnd 16 sc2 into next st, sc20, sc2 into next st (24)
Rnd 17 sc2 into next st, sc22, sc2 into next st (26)
Change to Charcoal.
Rnd 18 sc
Continue in Shale.
Rnds 19–21 sc (3 rnds)
Rnd 22 (sc11, sc2tog) twice (24)
Rnd 23 (sc2, sc2tog) 6 times (18)
Rnd 24 sc
Rnd 25 (sc1, sc2tog) 6 times (12)
Rnd 26 (sc2tog) 6 times (6)
Do not stuff.

BEAK
Working in Orange, begin by sc6 into ring.
Rnd 1 (sc2 into next st) 6 times (12)
Rnd 2 (sc1, sc2 into next st) 6 times (18)
Rnds 3–6 sc (4 rnds)
Rnd 7 (sc7, sc2tog) twice (16)
Rnd 8 sc
Rnd 9 (sc7, sc2 into next st) twice (18)
Rnd 10–13 sc (4 rnds)
Stuff lightly and sew into position.

TAIL
Working in Shale, ch18 and sl st to join into a circle.
Rnds 1–2 sc (2 rnds)
Change to Charcoal.
Rnd 3 (sc2, sc2 into next st) 6 times (24)
Change to Shale.
Rnd 4 sc
Split into three rnds of 8 sts and work each as follows:
Rnd 1 sc
Change to Charcoal.
Rnds 2–4 sc (3 rnds)
Rnd 5 (sc2tog) 4 times (4)
Do not stuff.

Finish by sewing eyes into place with Black yarn.

7

MARGOT
THE SWAN

Margot has been persuaded to come out of retirement to don her tutu one last time this Christmas. As a fundraiser for a high-profile charity, she'll perform her pirouetting finale in a star-studded performance of *The Nutcracker*. Masking any hints of arthritis as she retakes the spotlight after decades, she channels her teenage self as she prepares to play the first role she wore her pointe shoes on stage for. For once her poised and steely guard is down as she rehearses to plié again with the Mouse King with the memories of over five decades of watching other sugar plum fairies spinning around inside her mind.

SKILL LEVEL: EASY **CREAM, BLACK, ORANGE**

BODY/NECK/HEAD
Working in Cream, begin by sc6 into ring.
Rnd 1 (sc2 into next st) 6 times (12 sts)
Rnd 2 (sc1, sc2 into next st) 6 times (18)
Rnd 3 (sc2, sc2 into next st) 6 times (24)
Rnd 4 (sc3, sc2 into next st) 6 times (30)
Rnd 5 (sc4, sc2 into next st) 6 times (36)
Rnd 6 (sc5, sc2 into next st) 6 times (42)
Rnds 7–9 sc (3 rnds)
Rnd 10 (sc5, sc2tog) 6 times (36)
Rnds 11–14 sc (4 rnds)
Rnd 15 (sc4, sc2tog) 6 times (30)
Rnds 16–19 sc (4 rnds)
Rnd 20 (sc3, sc2tog) 6 times (24)
Rnd 21 sc
Rnd 22 (sc2tog) 9 times, sc6 (15)
Rnd 23 (sc2tog) 5 times, sc5 (10)
Rnds 24–29 sc (6 rnds)
Rnd 30 (sc2 into next st) 10 times (20)
Rnd 31 (sc3, sc2 into next st) 5 times (25)
Rnd 32 (sc4, sc2 into next st) 5 times (30)
Rnd 33 (sc2, sc2 into next st) 10 times (40)
Rnds 34–36 sc (3 rnds)
Rnd 37 (sc8, sc2tog) 4 times (36)
Rnd 38 sc
Rnd 39 (sc4, sc2tog) 6 times (30)
Rnd 40 (sc3, sc2tog) 6 times (24)
Rnd 41 (sc2, sc2tog) 6 times (18)
Rnd 42 sc
Rnd 43 (sc2tog) 9 times (9)
Rnd 44 (sc1, sc2tog) 3 times (6)

LEGS (make two)
Working in Cream, ch15 and sl st to join into a circle.
Rnds 1–2 sc (2 rnds)
Rnd 3 (sc3, sc2tog) 3 times (12)
Rnd 4 (sc2, sc2tog) 3 times (9)
Rnds 5–6 sc (2 rnds)
Rnd 7 (sc1, sc2tog) 3 times (6)
Change to Black.
Rnds 8–12 sc (5 rnds)
Rnd 13 (sc2 into next st) 6 times (12)
Rnds 14–15 sc (2 rnds)
Rnd 16 (sc2tog) 6 times (6)
Rnds 17–22 sc (6 rnds)
Rnd 23 (sc2 into next st) 6 times (12)
Rnd 24 sc
Rnd 25 (sc5, sc2 into next st) twice (14)
Rnd 26 (sc6, sc2 into next st) twice (16)
Rnd 27 (sc7, sc2 into next st) twice (18)
Rnds 28–32 sc (5 rnds)
Split into three rnds of 6 sts and work each as follows:
Rnd 1 sc
Rnd 2 (sc2tog) 3 times (3)
Lightly stuff thigh and sew flat across top to close.

WINGS (make two)
Working in Cream, begin by sc6 into ring.
Rnd 1 (sc2 into next st) 6 times (12)
Rnd 2 (sc1, sc2 into next st) 6 times (18)
Rnd 3 (sc2, sc2 into next st) 6 times (24)
Rnd 4 (sc3, sc2 into next st) 6 times (30)
Rnds 5–10 sc (6 rnds)

Split 10 sts and work as follows:
Rnds 1–4 sc (4 rnds)
Rnd 5 (sc2tog) 5 times (5)
Rejoin and work remaining 20 sts as follows:
Rnds 1–3 sc (3 rnds)
Rnd 4 sc5 (incomplete rnd)
Split into two rnds of 10 sts and work first 10-st rnd as follows:
Rnds 1–4 sc (4 rnds)
Rnd 5 (sc2tog) 5 times (5)
Rejoin and work final 10-st rnd as follows:
Rnds 1–6 sc (6 rnds)
Rnd 7 (sc2tog) 5 times (5)
Do not stuff.

BEAK
Working in Black, begin by sc6 into ring.
Change to Orange.
Rnd 1 (sc2 into next st) 6 times (12)
Rnd 2 (sc1, sc2 into next st) 6 times (18)
Rnds 3–5 sc (3 rnds)
Rnd 6 (sc4, sc2tog) 3 times (15)
Rnds 7–12 sc (6 rnds)
Change to Black.
Rnd 13 (sc4, sc2 into next st) 3 times (18)
Rnds 14–15 sc (2 rnds)
Rnd 16 (sc2, sc2 into next st) 6 times (24)
Stuff lightly and sew into position.

TAIL
Working in Cream, ch18 and sl st to join into a circle.
Rnd 1 sc
Rnd 2 (sc2, sc2 into next st) 6 times (24)
Rnd 3 (sc5, sc2 into next st) 4 times (28)
Split into three rnds with one rnd of 12 sts in the middle and two rnds of 8 sts either side. Work each 8-st rnd as follows:
Rnds 1–2 sc (2 rnds)
Rnd 3 (sc2tog) 4 times (4)
Rejoin and work the central 12-st rnd as follows:
Rnds 1–4 sc (4 rnds)
Rnd 5 (sc2, sc2tog) 3 times (9)
Rnd 6 (sc1, sc2tog) 3 times (6)
Rnd 7 (sc2tog) 3 times (3)
Do not stuff.

Finish by sewing eyes into place with Black yarn.

DELILAH
THE CATTLE EGRET

Known as somewhat of an eccentric throughout the entire village she lives in, Delilah is planning on really living up to her reputation this Christmas. She's embarking upon a culinary experiment of cooking the roast turkey on her award-winning shiny, new barbeque. Dissatisfied with the drizzly, underwhelming summer this year, she only scraped half a dozen chances to incinerate a few blocks of halloumi and so is desperate to turn her skills to something more challenging. With military precision she's meticulously calculated timings, temperatures, and seasoning, which she's confident will land dinner on the table at the perfect time for a morning stretch of the legs and a post-dinner snooze in front of the TV.

SKILL LEVEL: INTERMEDIATE **CREAM, CHARCOAL, YELLOW**

BODY/NECK/HEAD
Working in Cream, begin by sc6 into ring.
Rnd 1 (sc2 into next st) 6 times (12 sts)
Rnd 2 (sc1, sc2 into next st) 6 times (18)
Rnd 3 (sc2, sc2 into next st) 6 times (24)
Rnd 4 (sc3, sc2 into next st) 6 times (30)
Rnd 5 (sc4, sc2 into next st) 6 times (36)
Rnd 6 (sc5, sc2 into next st) 6 times (42)
Rnds 7–9 sc (3 rnds)
Rnd 10 (sc5, sc2tog) 6 times (36)
Rnds 11–14 sc (4 rnds)
Rnd 15 (sc4, sc2tog) 6 times (30)
Rnds 16–19 sc (4 rnds)
Rnd 20 (sc3, sc2tog) 6 times (24)
Rnd 21 sc
Rnd 22 (sc2tog) 9 times, sc6 (15)
Rnd 23 (sc2tog) 5 times, sc5 (10)
Stuff and continue.
Rnds 24–29 sc (6 rnds)
Rnd 30 (sc2 into next st) 10 times (20)
Rnd 31 (sc3, sc2 into next st) 5 times (25)
Work ½ inch (2 cm) LOOP STITCH (see page 17) every st as instructed.
Rnd 32 sc4, sc2 into next st, sc4 loop, sc2 into next st loop, (sc4, sc2 into next st) 3 times (30)
Rnd 33 (sc2, sc2 into next st) twice, (sc2 loop, sc2 into next st loop) twice, (sc2, sc2 into next st) 6 times (40)
Continue without loops.
Rnds 34–36 sc (3 rnds)
Rnd 37 (sc8, sc2tog) 4 times (36)

Rnd 38 sc
Rnd 39 (sc4, sc2tog) 6 times (30)
Rnd 40 (sc3, sc2tog) 6 times (24)
Rnd 41 (sc2, sc2tog) 6 times (18)
Rnd 42 sc
Rnd 43 (sc2tog) 9 times (9)
Rnd 44 (sc1, sc2tog) 3 times (6)

LEGS (make two)
Working in Cream, ch12 and sl st to join into a circle.
Rnds 1–3 sc (3 rnds)
Rnd 4 (sc2, sc2tog) 3 times (9)
Rnd 5 (sc1, sc2tog) 3 times (6)
Change to Yellow.
Rnds 6–14 sc (9 rnds)
Change to Charcoal.
Rnd 15 (sc2 into next st) 6 times (12)
Rnds 16–17 sc (2 rnds)
Rnd 18 (sc2tog) 6 times (6)
Rnds 19–28 sc (10 rnds)
Rnd 29 (sc2 into next st) 6 times (12)
Rnd 30 (sc1, sc2 into next st) 6 times (18)
Split into three rnds of 6 sts and work each as follows:
Rnds 1–4 sc (4 rnds)
Rnd 5 sc2tog, sc4 (5)
Rnds 6–7 sc (2 rnds)
Rnd 8 sc2tog, sc3 (4)
Rnd 9 (sc2tog) twice (2)

BACK DIGIT (optional)
SLIP STITCH TRAVERSE (see page 19) a 6-st root on the back of the foot and work as follows:
Rnds 1–2 sc (2 rnds)
Rnd 3 (sc2tog) 3 times (3)
Lightly stuff thigh and sew flat across top to close.

WINGS (make two)
Working in Cream, begin by sc6 into ring.
Rnd 1 (sc1, sc2 into next st) 3 times (9)
Rnd 2 sc8, sc2 into next st (10)
Rnd 3 sc
Rnd 4 sc9, sc2 into next st (11)
Rnd 5 sc
Rnd 6 sc10, sc2 into next st (12)
Rnd 7 sc
Rnd 8 sc11, sc2 into next st (13)
Rnd 9 sc
Rnd 10 sc12, sc2 into next st (14)
Rnd 11 sc
Rnd 12 (sc6, sc2 into next st) twice (16)
Rnd 13 sc2 into next st, sc14, sc2 into next st (18)
Rnd 14 sc2 into next st, sc16, sc2 into next st (20)
Rnd 15 sc2 into next st, sc18, sc2 into next st (22)
Rnd 16 sc2 into next st, sc20, sc2 into next st (24)
Rnd 17 sc2 into next st, sc22, sc2 into next st (26)
Rnds 18–21 sc (4 rnds)
Rnd 22 (sc11, sc2tog) twice (24)
Rnd 23 (sc2, sc2tog) 6 times (18)
Rnd 24 sc
Rnd 25 (sc1, sc2tog) 6 times (12)
Rnd 26 (sc2tog) 6 times (6)

BEAK
Working in Yellow, ch15 and sl st to join into a circle.
Rnds 1–5 sc (5 rnds)
Rnd 6 (sc3, sc2tog) 3 times (12)
Rnds 7–9 sc (3 rnds)
Rnd 10 (sc2, sc2tog) 3 times (9)
Change to Charcoal.
Rnds 11–13 sc (3 rnds)
Rnd 14 (sc1, sc2tog) 3 times (6)
Stuff lightly and sew into position.

EYES (make two)
Working in Yellow, begin by sc6 in ring.
Sew into position.

TAIL
Working in Cream, ch18 and sl st to join into a circle.
Rnds 1–3 sc (3 rnds)
Rnd 4 (sc2, sc2 into next st) 6 times (24)
Rnd 5 sc
Split into three rnds of 8 sts and work each as follows:
Rnds 1–7 sc (7 rnds)
Rnd 8 (sc2, sc2tog) twice (6)
Rnd 9 (sc2tog) 3 times (3)
Do not stuff.

Finish by sewing eyes into place with Black yarn.

9

LOIS
THE GREAT CORMORANT

Lois has woken up with regrets following one too many at her office party last night. Quite predictably, once the bubbles started pouring and she started rocking around the Christmas tree, her sensible plan to just have one and then drive herself home went out the window. She surprised herself with her dominance on the dance floor this year, waddling out all her best moves once the disco tunes replaced the Christmas party mix. Dragging herself into a boiling hot shower, she wonders: Why didn't she eat more canapés? Was the last song of the night really THAT track? Why did she decide to share the taxi home? Does she really now have to go and get the bus? Who knows what gossip she might face around the coffee machine . . .

SKILL LEVEL: INTERMEDIATE **CHARCOAL, CREAM, YELLOW, OATMEAL**

BODY/NECK/HEAD
Working in Charcoal, begin by sc6 into ring.
Rnd 1 (sc2 into next st) 6 times (12 sts)
Rnd 2 (sc1, sc2 into next st) 6 times (18)
Rnd 3 (sc2, sc2 into next st) 6 times (24)
Rnd 4 (sc3, sc2 into next st) 6 times (30)
Rnd 5 (sc4, sc2 into next st) 6 times (36)
Rnd 6 (sc5, sc2 into next st) 6 times (42)
Rnds 7–9 sc (3 rnds)
Rnd 10 (sc5, sc2tog) 6 times (36)
Rnds 11–14 sc (4 rnds)
Rnd 15 (sc4, sc2tog) 6 times (30)
Rnds 16–19 sc (4 rnds)
Rnd 20 (sc3, sc2tog) 6 times (24)
Rnd 21 sc
Rnd 22 (sc2tog) 9 times, sc6 (15)
Rnd 23 (sc2tog) 5 times, sc5 (10)
Stuff and continue.
Rnds 24–28 sc (5 rnds)
Rnd 29 (sc2 into next st) 10 times (20)
Rnd 30 (sc3, sc2 into next st) 5 times (25)
Rnd 31 (sc4, sc2 into next st) 5 times (30)
Rnd 32 (sc2, sc2 into next st) 10 times (40)
Rnds 33–35 sc5 Charcoal, sc5 Cream, sc10 Yellow, sc5 Cream, sc15 Charcoal (3 rnds)
Rnd 36 sc5 Charcoal, sc3, sc2tog Cream, sc8, sc2tog Yellow, sc5 Cream, sc3, sc2tog, sc8, sc2tog Charcoal (36)
Rnd 37 sc5 Charcoal, sc4 Cream, sc9 Yellow, sc5 Cream, sc13 Charcoal
Continue in Charcoal.
Rnd 38 (sc4, sc2tog) 6 times (30)
Rnd 39 (sc3, sc2tog) 6 times (24)
Rnd 40 (sc2, sc2tog) 6 times (18)
Rnd 41 sc
Rnd 42 (sc2tog) 9 times (9)
Rnd 43 (sc1, sc2tog) 3 times (6)

LEGS (make two)
Working in Cream, ch16 and sl st to join into a circle.
Rnds 1–5 sc (5 rnds)
Rnd 6 (sc2, sc2tog) 4 times (12)
Rnd 7 (sc1, sc2tog) 4 times (8)
Change to Charcoal.
Rnds 8–9 sc (2 rnds)
Rnd 10 (sc1, sc2 into next st) 4 times (12)
Rnds 11–12 sc (2 rnds)
Rnd 13 (sc1, sc2tog) 4 times (8)
Rnds 14–20 sc (7 rnds)
Rnd 21 (sc2 into next st) 8 times (16)
Rnd 22 sc
Rnd 23 (sc7, sc2 into next st) twice (18)
Rnd 24 (sc8, sc2 into next st) twice (20)
Rnd 25 sc
Rnd 26 (sc9, sc2 into next st) twice (22)
Rnd 27 sc
Rnd 28 (sc10, sc2 into next st) twice (24)
Rnds 29–31 sc (3 rnds)
Split into three rnds of 8 sts and work each as follows:
Rnd 1 sc
Rnd 2 (sc2tog) 4 times (4)
Rnd 3 (sc2tog) twice (2)

BACK DIGIT (optional)
SLIP STITCH TRAVERSE (see page 19) a 6-st root on back of foot and work as follows:
Rnd 1 sc
Rnd 2 sc2tog, sc4 (5)
Rnd 3 sc
Rnd 4 sc2tog, sc3 (4)
Lightly stuff thigh and sew flat across top to close.

WINGS (make two)
Working in Charcoal, begin by sc6 into ring.
Rnd 1 (sc1, sc2 into next st) 3 times (9)
Rnd 2 sc8, sc2 into next st (10)
Rnd 3 sc
Rnd 4 sc9, sc2 into next st (11)
Rnd 5 sc
Rnd 6 sc10, sc2 into next st (12)
Rnd 7 sc
Rnd 8 sc11, sc2 into next st (13)
Rnd 9 sc
Rnd 10 sc12, sc2 into next st (14)
Rnd 11 sc
Rnd 12 (sc6, sc2 into next st) twice (16)
Rnd 13 sc2 into next st, sc14, sc2 into next st (18)
Rnd 14 sc2 into next st, sc16, sc2 into next st (20)
Rnd 15 sc2 into next st, sc18, sc2 into next st (22)
Rnd 16 sc2 into next st, sc20, sc2 into next st (24)
Rnd 17 sc2 into next st, sc22, sc2 into next st (26)
Rnds 18–21 sc (4 rnds)
Rnd 22 (sc11, sc2tog) twice (24)
Rnd 23 (sc2, sc2tog) 6 times (18)
Rnd 24 sc
Rnd 25 (sc1, sc2tog) 6 times (12)
Rnd 26 (sc2tog) 6 times (6)
Do not stuff.

BEAK
Working in Oatmeal, ch15 and sl st to join into a circle.
Rnds 1–8 sc (8 rnds)
Rnd 9 (sc3, sc2tog) 3 times (12)
Rnds 10–12 sc (3 rnds)
Rnd 13 (sc2, sc2tog) 3 times (9)
Rnd 14 sc
Rnd 15 (sc1, sc2tog) 3 times (6)
Stuff lightly and sew into position.

TAIL
Working in Charcoal, ch18 and sl st to join into a circle.
Rnds 1–3 sc (3 rnds)
Rnd 4 (sc2, sc2 into next st) 6 times (24)
Rnd 5 sc
Split into three rnds of 8 sts and work each as follows:
Rnds 1–6 sc (6 rnds)
Rnd 7 sc2 into next st, sc7 (9)
Rnds 8–11 sc (4 rnds)
Rnd 12 (sc1, sc2tog) 3 times (6)
Do not stuff.

Finish by sewing eyes into place with Black yarn.

10

AGNES
THE HERON

It was the night before Christmas, and Agnes flopped down onto the middle of her sofa and crossed her long legs as she put her feet up on the coffee-table. We all know that the festive season can be a busy time, but this year Agnes certainly deserves far more than a lump of coal in her stocking. Between school nativity plays, shopping lists, endless "get-togethers," and very difficult logistics planning to get all her elderly relatives in the right place for tonight, she is feeling frazzled. Resting her head back on the sofa and closing her eyes just for a second, she takes a long deep breath, enjoys a moment of silence, and smiles when she thinks about the children's faces in the morning.

SKILL LEVEL: EASY **SILVER, OATMEAL, CREAM, CAMEL, BLACK**

BODY/NECK/HEAD
Working in Silver, begin by sc6 into ring.
Rnd 1 (sc2 into next st) 6 times (12 sts)
Rnd 2 (sc1, sc2 into next st) 6 times (18)
Rnd 3 (sc2, sc2 into next st) 6 times (24)
Rnd 4 (sc3, sc2 into next st) 6 times (30)
Rnd 5 (sc4, sc2 into next st) 6 times (36)
Rnd 6 (sc5, sc2 into next st) 6 times (42)
Rnds 7–9 sc (3 rnds)
Rnd 10 (sc5, sc2tog) 6 times (36)
Rnds 11–14 sc (4 rnds)
Rnd 15 (sc4, sc2tog) 6 times (30)
Rnds 16–19 sc (4 rnds)
Rnd 20 (sc3, sc2tog) 6 times (24)
Rnd 21 sc
Rnd 22 (sc2tog) 9 times, sc6 (15)
Rnd 23 (sc2tog) 5 times, sc5 (10)
Change to Cream.
Rnds 24–31 sc (8 rnds)
Rnd 32 (sc2 into next st) 10 times (20)
Rnd 33 (sc3, sc2 into next st) 5 times (25)
Rnd 34 (sc4, sc2 into next st) 5 times (30)
Rnd 35 (sc2, sc2 into next st) 10 times (40)
Rnds 36–38 sc (3 rnds)
Rnd 39 (sc8, sc2tog) 4 times (36)
Rnd 40 sc
Rnd 41 (sc4, sc2tog) 6 times (30)
Rnd 42 (sc3, sc2tog) 6 times (24)
Rnd 43 (sc2, sc2tog) 6 times (18)
Rnd 44 sc

Rnd 45 (sc2tog) 9 times (9)
Rnd 46 (sc1, sc2tog) 3 times (6)

LEGS (make two)
Working in Silver, ch12 and sl st to join into a circle.
Rnds 1–3 sc (3 rnds)
Rnd 4 (sc2, sc2tog) 3 times (9)
Rnd 5 (sc1, sc2tog) 3 times (6)
Change to Oatmeal.
Rnds 6–14 sc (9 rnds)
Rnd 15 (sc2 into next st) 6 times (12)
Rnds 16–17 sc (2 rnds)
Rnd 18 (sc2tog) 6 times (6)
Rnds 19–28 sc (10 rnds)
Rnd 29 (sc2 into next st) 6 times (12)
Rnd 30 (sc1, sc2 into next st) 6 times (18)
Split into three rounds of 6 sts and work each as follows:
Rnds 1–4 sc (4 rnds)
Rnd 5 sc2tog, sc4 (5)
Rnds 6–7 sc (2 rnds)
Rnd 8 sc2tog, sc3 (4)
Rnd 9 (sc2tog) twice (2)
Lightly stuff thigh.

BACK DIGIT (optional)
SLIP STITCH TRAVERSE (see page 19) a 6-st root on back of foot and work as follows:
Rnds 1–2 sc (2 rnds)
Rnd 3 (sc2tog) 3 times (3)

WINGS (make two)
Working in Silver, begin by sc6 into ring.
Rnd 1 (sc1, sc2 into next st) 3 times (9)
Rnd 2 sc8, sc2 into next st (10)
Rnd 3 sc
Rnd 4 sc9, sc2 into next st (11)
Rnd 5 sc
Rnd 6 sc10, sc2 into next st (12)
Rnd 7 sc
Rnd 8 sc11, sc2 into next st (13)
Rnd 9 sc
Rnd 10 sc12, sc2 into next st (14)
Rnd 11 sc
Rnd 12 (sc6, sc2 into next st) twice (16)
Rnd 13 sc2 into next st, sc14, sc2 into next st (18)
Rnd 14 sc2 into next st, sc16, sc2 into next st (20)
Rnd 15 sc2 into next st, sc18, sc2 into next st (22)
Rnd 16 sc2 into next st, sc20, sc2 into next st (24)
Rnd 17 sc2 into next st, sc22, sc2 into next st (26)
Rnds 18–21 sc (4 rnds)
Rnd 22 (sc11, sc2tog) twice (24)
Rnd 23 (sc2, sc2tog) 6 times (18)
Rnd 24 sc
Rnd 25 (sc1, sc2tog) 6 times (12)
Rnd 26 (sc2tog) 6 times (6)
Do not stuff.

BEAK
Working in Camel, ch18 and sl st to join into a circle.
Rnds 1–4 sc (4 rnds)
Rnd 5 (sc4, sc2tog) 3 times (15)
Rnds 6–8 sc (3 rnds)

Rnd 9 (sc3, sc2tog) 3 times (12)
Rnds 10–11 sc (2 rnds)
Rnd 12 (sc2, sc2tog) 3 times (9)
Rnds 13–14 sc (2 rnds)
Rnd 15 (sc1, sc2tog) 3 times (6)
Stuff lightly and sew into position.

TAIL
Working in Silver, ch18 and sl st to join into circle.
Rnds 1–2 sc (2 rnds)
Rnd 3 (sc2, sc2 into next st) 6 times (24)
Rnd 4 sc
Change to Black.
Split into three rnds of 8 sts and work each as follows:
Rnds 1–4 sc (4 rnds)
Rnd 5 (sc2tog) 4 times (4)

CREST
Working in Black, SLIP STITCH TRAVERSE (see page 18) 8 sts from front of head to back, then work one ch18 SLIP STITCH CHAIN (see page 19). Repeat on opposite side of head.

Finish by sewing eyes into place with Black yarn.

11

NINA
THE SPOON-BILLED SANDPIPER

Nina is counting down the last few hours at work until she can throw an armful of clothes onto the back seat of her hatchback and hit the long road home for Christmas. Although reluctant to ever admit it, she's been more than just a little homesick these last few months and is longing for some of her mom's cooking, the smell of freshly laundered sheets and the early-morning cup of tea that appears at her bedside at exactly the right temperature as she opens her eyes. Her first semester at university has been a little different from what she had expected, and for the first time ever, she's actually looking forward to filling up her dinner plate with veggies (and might go as far as to enjoy a couple of Brussels sprouts!).

SKILL LEVEL: INTERMEDIATE　　　　　　　　　　　　　　　　　　　　**CREAM, CHESTNUT, STONE**

BODY/NECK/HEAD
Working in Cream, begin by sc6 into ring.
Rnd 1 (sc2 into next st) 6 times (12 sts)
Rnd 2 (sc1, sc2 into next st) 6 times (18)
Rnd 3 (sc2, sc2 into next st) 6 times (24)
Rnd 4 (sc3, sc2 into next st) 6 times (30)
Rnd 5 (sc4, sc2 into next st) 6 times (36)
Rnd 6 (sc5, sc2 into next st) 6 times (42)
Rnds 7–9 sc (3 rnds)
Rnd 10 (sc5, sc2tog) 6 times (36)
Rnds 11–14 sc (4 rnds)
Rnd 15 (sc4, sc2tog) 6 times (30)
Rnds 16–19 sc (4 rnds)
Rnd 20 (sc3, sc2tog) 6 times (24)
Rnd 21 sc
Rnd 22 (sc2tog) 9 times, sc6 (15)
Rnd 23 (sc2tog) 5 times, sc5 (10)
Stuff and continue.
Rnd 24 sc
Rnd 25 (sc2 into next st) 10 times (20)
Rnd 26 (sc3, sc2 into next st) 5 times (25)
Rnd 27 (sc4, sc2 into next st) 5 times (30)
Rnd 28 (sc2, sc2 into next st) 10 times (40)
Rnds 29–31 sc (3 rnds)
Rnd 32 (sc8, sc2tog) 4 times (36)
Rnd 33 sc
Change to Stone.
Rnd 34 (sc4, sc2tog) 6 times (30)
Continue in Stone with every 4th st in Chestnut.
Rnd 35 (sc3, sc2tog) 6 times (24)
Rnd 36 (sc2, sc2tog) 6 times (18)
Rnd 37 sc
Rnd 38 (sc2tog) 9 times (9)
Rnd 39 (sc1, sc2tog) 3 times (6)

LEGS (make two)
Working in Cream, ch12 and sl st to join into a circle.
Rnds 1–3 sc (3 rnds)
Rnd 4 (sc2, sc2tog) 3 times (9)
Rnd 5 (sc1, sc2tog) 3 times (6)
Change to Chestnut.
Rnds 6–12 sc (7 rnds)
Rnd 13 (sc2 into next st) 6 times (12)
Rnds 14–15 sc (2 rnds)
Rnd 16 (sc2tog) 6 times (6)
Rnds 17–24 sc (8 rnds)
Rnd 25 (sc2 into next st) 6 times (12)
Rnd 26 (sc1, sc2 into next st) 6 times (18)
Split into three rnds of 6 sts and work each as follows:
Rnds 1–5 sc (5 rnds)
Rnd 6 sc2tog, sc4 (5)
Rnds 7–8 sc (2 rnds)
Rnd 9 sc2tog, sc3 (4)

BACK DIGIT (optional)
SLIP STITCH TRAVERSE (see page 19) a 6-st root on the back of the foot and work as follows:
Rnds 1–4 sc (4 rnds)
Rnd 5 (sc2tog) 3 times (3)
Lightly stuff thigh and sew flat across top to close.

85

WINGS (make two)

Working in Stone with every 4th st in Chestnut, begin by sc6 into ring.

Rnd 1 (sc1, sc2 into next st) 3 times (9)
Rnd 2 sc8, sc2 into next st (10)
Rnd 3 sc
Rnd 4 sc9, sc2 into next st (11)
Rnd 5 sc
Rnd 6 sc10, sc2 into next st (12)
Rnd 7 sc
Rnd 8 sc11, sc2 into next st (13)
Rnd 9 sc
Rnd 10 sc12, sc2 into next st (14)
Rnd 11 sc
Rnd 12 (sc6, sc2 into next st) twice (16)
Rnd 13 sc2 into next st, sc14, sc2 into next st (18)
Rnd 14 sc2 into next st, sc16, sc2 into next st (20)
Rnd 15 sc2 into next st, sc18, sc2 into next st (22)
Rnd 16 sc2 into next st, sc20, sc2 into next st (24)
Rnd 17 sc2 into next st, sc22, sc2 into next st (26)
Rnds 18–21 sc (4 rnds)
Rnd 22 (sc11, sc2tog) twice (24)
Rnd 23 (sc2, sc2tog) 6 times (18)
Rnd 24 sc
Rnd 25 (sc1, sc2tog) 6 times (12)
Rnd 26 (sc2tog) 6 times (6)
Do not stuff.

BEAK

Working in Chestnut, begin by sc6 into ring.

Rnd 1 (sc2 into next st) 6 times (12)
Rnds 2–4 sc (3 rnds)
Rnd 5 (sc1, sc2tog) 4 times (8)
Rnds 6–13 sc (8 rnds)
Rnd 14 (sc3, sc2 into next st) twice (10)
Rnd 15 (sc4, sc2 into next st) twice (12)
Stuff top section lightly and sew flat into position.

TAIL

Working in Cream, ch16 and sl st to join into a circle.
Change to Stone with every 4th st in Chestnut.
Rnds 1–6 sc (6 rnds)
Split into two rnds of 8 sts and work each as follows:
Rnds 1–4 sc (4 rnds)
Rnd 5 sc7, sc2 into next st (9)
Rnds 6–7 sc (2 rnds)
Rnd 8 sc8, sc2 into next st (10)
Rnds 9–10 sc (2 rnds)
Continue in Chestnut.
Rnd 11 (sc4, sc2 into next st) twice (12)
Rnds 12–13 sc (2 rnds)
Rnd 14 (sc2tog) 6 times (6)
Do not stuff.

Finish by sewing eyes into place with Black yarn.

12

JOHN
THE SPOTTED WOODPECKER

Christmas is a very serious business when you live in the UK's number one "festive zip code." On the stroke of midnight on November 30, John has the pleasure of twisting the last twinkling bulb into place, and over two hundred thousand flashing lights start to spread cheer to everyone who sees them. It all started when he moved next door to his now best pal Dave, and they had a chat over the fence about plans for putting a few lights in the hedge between their houses. It rapidly became apparent that he'd opportunely moved to a street full of people just as enthusiastic about LEDs as he is, and a couple of years, and miles and miles of lights later, they were attracting visitors from across the county.
Every year, on January 6 (and not a moment too soon), they come back down, and he returns to a frugal lifestyle as he spends a year saving to afford the electricity bill for next December!

SKILL LEVEL: INTERMEDIATE   **CREAM, BLACK, RUBY, STEEL**

BODY/NECK/HEAD

Work as Spoon-Bill BODY (page 85) starting in Ruby and changing to Cream after rnd 7 then to Black after rnd 24.

Rnd 25 (sc2 into next st) 10 times (20)
Rnd 26 (sc3, sc2 into next st) 5 times (25)
Rnd 27 (sc4, sc2 into next st) 5 times (30)
Rnd 28 (sc2, sc2 into next st) 5 times Ruby, (sc2, sc2 into next st) 5 times Cream (40)
Rnd 29–31 sc20 Ruby, sc20 Cream (3 rnds)
Rnd 32 (sc8, sc2tog) twice Ruby, (sc8, sc2tog) twice Cream (36)
Rnd 33 sc18 Ruby, sc18 Cream
Rnd 34 (sc4, sc2tog) 3 times Ruby, (sc4, sc2tog) 3 times Cream (30)
Change to Black.
Rnd 35 (sc3, sc2tog) 6 times (24)
Rnd 36 (sc2, sc2tog) 6 times (18)
Rnd 37 sc
Rnd 38 (sc2tog) 9 times (9)
Rnd 39 (sc1, sc2tog) 3 times (6)

LEGS (make two)

Working in Ruby, ch12 and sl st to join into a circle.
Change to Cream.
Rnds 1–8 sc (8 rnds)
Rnd 9 (sc2tog) 6 times (6)
Change to Steel.
Rnds 10–18 sc (9 rnds)
Next, ch6 and sl st halfway across to other side of rnd to form two 8-st rnds (2 from rnd, 6 on chain). Work each rnd as follows:
Rnd 1 sc (8)
Rnd 2 (sc1, sc2 into next st) 4 times (12)
Split into two rnds of 6 sts and work each as follows:
Rnds 1–4 sc (4 rnds)
Rnd 5 (sc2, sc2 into next st) twice (8)
Rnds 6–7 sc (2 rnds)
Rnd 8 (sc2, sc2tog) twice (6)
Rnd 9 (sc1, sc2tog) twice (4)
Rnd 10 (sc2tog) twice (2)
Lightly stuff thigh and sew flat across top to close.

RIGHT WING

Working in Black, begin by sc6 into ring.
Rnd 1 (sc1, sc2 into next st) 3 times (9)
Change to Cream.
Rnd 2 sc8, sc2 into next st (10)
Rnd 3 sc
Change to Black.
Rnd 4 sc9, sc2 into next st (11)
Rnd 5 sc
Change to Cream.
Rnd 6 sc10, sc2 into next st (12)
Rnd 7 sc
Change to Black.
Rnd 8 sc11, sc2 into next st (13)
Rnd 9 sc
Rnd 10 sc7 Black, sc4 Cream, sc1, sc2 into next st Black (14)
Rnd 11 sc7 Black, sc4 Cream, sc3 Black
Rnd 12 sc6, sc2 into next st Black, sc4 Cream, sc2, sc2

into next st Black (16)

Rnd 13 sc2 into next st, sc7 Black, sc4 Cream, sc3, sc2 into next st Black (18)

Rnd 14 sc2 into next st, sc8 Black, sc4 Cream, sc4, sc2 into next st Black (20)

Rnd 15 sc2 into next st, sc9 Black, sc4 Cream, sc5, sc2 into next st Black (22)

Rnd 16 sc2 into next st, sc10 Black, sc4 Cream, sc6, sc2 into next st Black (24)

Rnd 17 sc2 into next st, sc11 Black, sc4 Cream, sc7, sc2 into next st Black (26)

Rnds 18–22 sc13 Black, sc4 Cream, sc9 Black (5 rnds)

Change to Black.

Rnd 23 (sc11, sc2tog) twice (24)

Rnd 24 (sc2, sc2tog) 6 times (18)

Change to Cream.

Rnd 25 sc

Rnd 26 (sc1, sc2tog) 6 times (12)

Rnd 27 (sc2tog) 6 times (6)

Do not stuff.

LEFT WING

Work as RIGHT WING until:

Rnd 10 sc2 Black, sc4 Cream, sc6, sc2 into next st Black (14)

Rnd 11 sc2 Black, sc4 Cream, sc8 Black

Rnd 12 sc2 Black, sc4 Cream, sc2 into next st Black, sc6, sc2 into next st Black (16)

Rnd 13 sc2 into next st, sc1 Black, sc4 Cream, sc9, sc2 into next st Black (18)

Rnd 14 sc2 into next st, sc2 Black, sc4 Cream, sc10, sc2 into next st Black (20)

Rnd 15 sc2 into next st, sc3 Black, sc4 Cream, sc11, sc2 into next st Black (22)

Rnd 16 sc2 into next st, sc4 Black, sc4 Cream, sc12, sc2 into next st Black (24)

Rnd 17 sc2 into next st, sc5 Black, sc4 Cream, sc13, sc2 into next st Black (26)

Rnds 18–22 sc7 Black, sc4 Cream, sc15 Black (5 rnds)

Continue as RIGHT WING.

BEAK

Working in Steel, ch12 and sl st to join into a circle.

Rnds 1–6 sc (6 rnds)

Rnd 7 (sc2, sc2tog) 3 times (9)

Rnds 8–9 sc (2 rnds)

Rnd 10 (sc1, sc2tog) 3 times (6)

Rnds 11–12 sc (2 rnds)

Stuff lightly and sew flat into position.

HEAD PLUMAGE

Working in Black, work three ch8 SLIP STITCH CHAINS (see page 19) onto top of head.

TAIL

Working in Ruby, ch16 and sl st to join into a circle.

Rnds 1–4 sc (4 rnds)

Change to Black.

Rnds 5–6 sc (2 rnds)

Split into two rnds of 8 sts and work both as follows:

Rnds 1–4 sc (4 rnds)

Rnd 5 sc7, sc2 into next st (9)

Rnds 6–8 sc (3 rnds)

Rnd 9 sc8, sc2 into next st (10)

Rnds 10–12 sc (3 rnds)

Rnd 13 (sc4, sc2 into next st) twice (12)

Rnds 14–16 sc (3 rnds)

Rnd 17 (sc2tog) 6 times (6)

Do not stuff.

Finish by sewing eyes into place with Black yarn.

ACKNOWLEDGMENTS

The birds for this book have been crocheted by a few sets of hands as we put our Christmas sweaters on, watched our favorite festive films, and maybe ate a mince pie or two.

With huge thanks to the talented Evelyn Birch, for capturing my hands in these step-by-step illustrations, and for all her assistance making this book by sawing down Christmas trees and putting up lights in February.

With special thanks to Jo Clements, Evelyn Birch, and Rachel Critchley in enabling me to suddenly fly way beyond the four calling birds!

Further thanks are due to the rest of the TOFT team in supporting my creativity and delivering an exceptional experience to all of TOFT's customers around the world.

As ever, I could not continue to run a business and find time to develop books and have two young children without the understanding and support of my parents and Doug Lord.

A final thanks to my children for continuing to inspire me every day.

ABOUT THE AUTHOR

Kerry Lord is the founder of TOFT, a dynamic British yarn brand specializing in luxury wools and approachable patterns. Initially established with a focus on fashion-led knitting kits, Kerry first created the super-popular Edward's Menagerie series of books in 2012, which have encouraged and taught thousands around the world to crochet for the first time.

TOFT continues to offer a strong design collection for both knitting and crochet; a commanding presence at craft shows all over the world, sold-out pattern subscription boxes (shipping internationally), and regular workshops at their Studio HQ in Warwickshire make TOFT a big part of the contemporary craft scene, both in the UK and across the world.

Kerry enjoys collaborating and cohosting ever-larger crochet events to bring new people to the craft, such as teaching 350 workshop attendees to make a whale at the Natural History Museum, London, and organizing a touring exhibition of over 500 crochet animals that bring together the wider range in Edward's Menagerie.

TOFT is here to help if you are new to crochet and not sure where to begin, and the brand is based from a real place called Toft in Warwickshire, England. In addition to yarns, TOFT now designs and manufactures a whole range of tools and accessories to accompany its crochet range.

Learn more about TOFT at www.toftuk.com, @toft_uk, and #edsanimals.

New York

An Imprint of Sterling Publishing Co., Inc.

LARK CRAFTS and the distinctive Lark logo are registered trademarks of Sterling Publishing Co., Inc.

Text and patterns/projects © 2020 Kerry Lord
Cover and photography © 2020 Pavilion Books Company Ltd

All rights reserved. No part of this publication may be reproduced, stored in a retrieval system, or transmitted in any form or by any means (including electronic, mechanical, photocopying, recording, or otherwise) without prior written permission from the publisher.

First published in the UK in 2020 by Pavilion Books Company Ltd

ISBN 978-1-4547-1142-1

Distributed in Canada by Sterling Publishing Co., Inc.
c/o Canadian Manda Group, 664 Annette Street
Toronto, Ontario M6S 2C8, Canada

For information about custom editions, special sales, and premium and corporate purchases, please contact Sterling Special Sales at 800-805-5489 or specialsales@sterlingpublishing.com.

Manufactured in Singapore

2 4 6 8 10 9 7 5 3 1

sterlingpublishing.com/larkcrafts

Photography by Kristy Noble